THIS BOOK BELONGS TO:

NAME: _____

_____

AGE: _____

D1372611

THE SECOND CAPTAINS SPORTS ANNUAL
Volume 1.
By Second Captains

Published by Second Captains.

A WELCOME FROM SECOND CAPTAINS

Dear Second Captaineers,

Welcome to the **Second Captains Sports Annual, Volume 1**. Back in 2008, after a particularly inane question from journalist Ken Early, Steve Staunton sneered out the words "second captain, first captain, whatever…"

We immediately knew we'd one day release a book inspired by those words, and seven years later, here we are.

"You can't be all things to all people", the saying goes – and yet, this book manages to do just that. Regardless of gender, age, sexual preference or ethnicity, the magnum opus you hold in your hand is the book you've been waiting for your entire life. Well, your entire life SINCE you stopped reading sports annuals as a child.

We would describe The Second Captains Sports Annual Volume 1 as a heady cocktail of quality sports writing and absolute bullshit. We have contributions from US Murph, cartoonist David Squires, Jerry Izenberg, Damien Duff, and from PBESOers across the world.

We attempt to answer the deepest questions in Irish sport – why is Conor McGregor so popular? What price a sportsperson's independence from big business? And what **REALLY** happened to Ken's football career in Marseille?

Mostly we just hope you enjoy it. The articles, the photos, the sillier bits… it's all inspired by what you lovely people send into us, and what you react to online. Consider this the minutes of our meetings with you since 2013.

Thank you all so much for your support of Second Captains, and sorry for all the cursing Mammy.

Sexily yours,

Eoin, Mark, Ken, Murph, and Simon.

CONTENTS

FOREWORD

BY

OLUWASHINA OKELEJI

Coach!

As one of the cult heroes of the famous Second Captains podcast, I have been invited by the boys to write a short welcome to this, **The Second Captains Sports Annual Volume 1.**

I have been told that my interview with former Nigeria coach Stephen Keshi during the World Cup of 2014 is played on a weekly basis on the podcast. For me, this either shows an appreciation of brave broadcast journalism, or a stifling inability by Second Captains to generate new, original content. Either way, I am honoured that the Irish people have taken me to their hearts.

I hope you encounter brave, direct, Oluwashina-style questioning not only throughout this book, but in future Irish sports broadcasting. Just imagine if Clifton Hugh Lancelot de Verdon Wrottesley, after finishing just outside the medals for Ireland in the skeleton at the Salt Lake City Winter Olympics of 2002, was asked, "Where do you think you got it all wrong today?". Or, after his defeat in UFC Fight Night 54 to Chris 'The Greek Assassin' Kelades, Irish hero Paddy 'The Hooligan' Holohan was forced to answer "You wanted victory but it didn't happen, what happened?" I hope you get the journalism you deserve.

Enjoy, my Irish friends.

Oluwashina Okeleji

SECTION 1

TERRY
MONAGHAN
THE EARLY
YEARS...

At home with
David O'Doherty

SEE INSIDE THE HOMES OF YOUR FAVOURITE STARS!

DAVID O'DOHERTY IS IRELAND'S BIGGEST CELEBRITY. TODAY HE ENTERTAINS THE WORLD IN COMEDY STAND-UP FORM, BUT IN HIS EARLIER YEARS, HIS 'SET' CONTAINED NOTHING BUT MAGNIFICENT OUTSIDE BREAKS, PROBING CORNER-BOUND SPIRAL KICKS AND PRECISE GARRYOWENS. HE WAS A FINE ATTACKING FULL-BACK, BREEZING TO JUNIOR CUP GLORY IN 1991 AND WIDELY TIPPED AS THE SUCCESSOR TO JIM STAPLES' THRONE. WHICH TODAY BEGS THE QUESTION — WHAT DOES HE SPEND ALL HIS MONEY ON? LET'S FIND OUT! WELCOME INSIDE THE HOUSE OF COMEDY SHARP-SHOOTER DAVID O'DOHERTY!

1.

When he's not hitting laughter home-runs, he enjoys nothing more than indulging his competitive side. Watch as he displays his awesome Rugby Subbuteo skills. David drops in to the pocket for this attempted drop-goal. If football is a gentleman's game played by thugs, and rugby a thug's game played by gentlemen, then rugby Subbuteo is a mug's game, played by giant-handed 6 foot 2 comedians. Keep that scoreboard ticking over David!

2.

WINNER! WINNER! WINNER!

But it's not just in the make-believe world of rugby Subbuteo that David excels – he can also produce the goods in the white-hot heat of battle. Here is his 1990 East Leinster Under-14 triple jump bronze medal – a tasty *hors d'oeuvre* to 1991's meaty Junior Cup *entrée*.

3.

Lance Armstrong was once David's sporting hero – here's some saddle cream he bought at his bike shop in Austin, Texas. The ass rash disappeared but Lance's betrayal hurt him much more deeply. All he has left are memories... and VHS tapes of the 1987 Tour de France which he watches in his front room while cycling. He is also a vocal anti-doping campaigner. Go David Go!

4.

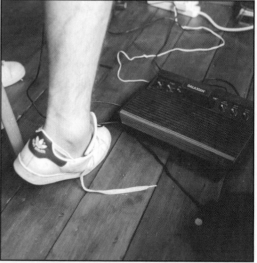

Computer games are popular now amongst many young people, and David is no different. It's the last word in technical wizardry. You don't manually manipulate the figures in question here, they are controlled using these 'controllers'. David always competes wearing his "gaming cape" and his favourite computerized games include *Galaxian*, *Missile Command* and *Gary Halpin's Leinster Rugby Challenge*.

5.

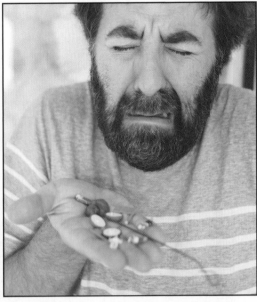

Everyone enjoys a game of Subbuteo now and then, here's David trying to muscle in on the action!! But we all know that those little guys are fragile... David counts the cost of another intensely physical battle. Don't cry David!

6.

Many people have called Alessandro Pirlo the 'slightly less-attractive David O'Doherty of Football.' They continue to inspire each other. When he's not doing massive comedy dumps in the bathroom, David enjoys looking back at his 1984 Panini Football Album – missing only Eric Black of Aberdeen (career stats – 96 goals in 265 games).

7.

Little-known fact alert – Arctic explorer Ernest Shackleton was a keen badmintoner, but all that gear really affected his backswing. David gets some practice in ahead of his gig (and super-secret badminton competition) in the Arctic Circle this December. Hit another winner David!

8.

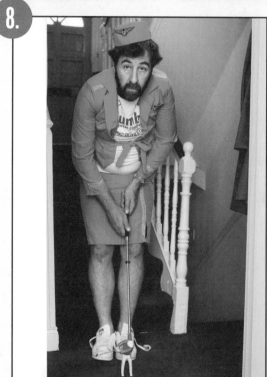

Golfwear is such a cliché that it can be hard to find a way to express your individuality. But our hero manages to confound expectations. Here's a mini Arnold Palmer that he found on his travels. FOOOOOOOOOOOORE!!!

THE FOOTBALLER'S LIFE
YOU CHOOSE THE MOVES!

OUR HERO

THE STORY OF TERRY MONAGHAN

ILLUSTRATIONS BY COLM MAC ATHLAOICH

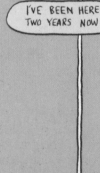

FOR HALF OF HIS LIFETIME, KEN EARLY HAS LOOKED UP
TO DAMIEN DUFF AS A HERO. SO HE WAS PRETTY EXCITED
WHEN DUFF AGREED TO MEET UP AND TALK ABOUT HIS LIFE
IN FOOTBALL – PAST, PRESENT AND FUTURE. WHEN THEY
FINALLY SAT DOWN TOGETHER IN A SOULLESS HOTEL BAR
NEAR DUBLIN AIRPORT, THERE WAS ONLY ONE QUESTION
ON DUFFER'S MIND. "WHAT EXACTLY IS THIS FOR AGAIN?"

Words: Ken Early

D Damien Duff is wondering what kind of book this is
supposed to be.

"It's supposed to be some kind of annual? Was it compared
to Buster or something?"

I try to explain what's going to be in this book, bits and bobs to
do with our show, a few longer pieces, one on Conor McGregor…

"Oh yeah? Going over to Vegas for that, a nice little gig. The
modern day Muhammad Ali! And he's Irish!"

I wonder if Duff is taking the piss. He and McGregor don't
immediately strike you as kindred spirits. But no, he's been a
McGregor fan since catching some episodes of *The Notorious*
during his recent stint in Melbourne.

"I was saying lads, come and have a look at this fucker. When his
Dad bowls in, you'd be in tears laughing at some of it. It was just
like watching *The Snapper*. But then he goes out and backs it up
doesn't he?"

Despite lacking McGregor's taste for the limelight, Duff has put
on some of the greatest shows I've ever seen from any Irish
sportsman. I was there in Suwon the night he was Ireland's
best player as they took Spain to penalties in the World Cup
second round. The sight of him twisting and turning the Spanish
defenders remains one of my most vivid football memories -
what does that night mean to him now?

"I had never watched any clips back until recently," he says. "Then
one of the lads - one of my school friends, we have a WhatsApp…

DUFFER

STREET FOOTBALLER

group - they threw it on two or three months ago, they were probably slagging me. But I had a look at it and… yeah, I actually did play well in that. Over the years a lot of people go, I was at the Spain game, you were great, you were this or you were that, but I'd never actually watched it back until then. I think it's just a couple of minutes on YouTube? So I watched that a few weeks ago and… yeah… I done alright I guess."

"I done alright" is a typically Duff description of what was probably the best individual performance in Ireland's World Cup history. The only other candidate would be Paul McGrath against Italy in Giants' Stadium. McGrath too would probably describe his performance that day as "alright". Ireland produces plenty of humble footballers. But we don't produce many like Duff - pacey dribblers who beat opponents and get the crowd on their feet. I wonder how he thinks he got that way.

"All I did was literally play football on the street every minute of the day. I keep hearing about coaches, but for me it's about learning on the street, and loving it. You need luck on your side, you have to be given a body that can take the workload. But I'm a big believer in hours. If you've got a young lad that's playing GAA two nights a week, hurling two nights a week and football one night a week… well, he's never really gonna be a footballer. He might give it

a go and all, but it's just never really gonna happen for him. So literally every night of the week and all day, whenever I got a chance, I'd play football."

"You can say the same about Robbie. A different type of footballer, but he's still a street footballer, Shay, Richie Dunne, the likes of that, just putting in hours every day, that's all they did. And I just don't see that now at all. I've done an awful lot of

I KEEP HEARING ABOUT COACHES, BUT FOR ME IT'S ABOUT LEARNING ON THE STREET, AND LOVING IT.

rehab recently on pitches down at Leicester [Celtic] and Marlay Park and you just don't see kids out playing football. It's obviously different nowadays, mas and das don't let them out on the street.

But at Rovers, I'm coaching the U15 lads, and it's like 'What ya do last night?' Instead of playing football they're playing each other in FIFA. I'm trying to tell them, you're not gonna get good at dribbling or scoring goals or kicking with your left and your right if you're playing FIFA. It's ridiculous.

"So I'll try and hold off with my kids as long as possible for Facebook, Twitter… phones… cause it's not the way I was brought up. Then again, if they don't have their PlayStation or their phone or whatever when they're ten or eleven they're probably getting picked on in school. I guess it's a Catch-22. But I don't think the kids put the hours in any more.

"I can't even remember when I started - four or five, I dunno. It's a bit worrying when you look at the other end of it, when I finish, what else have I got? I can go into coaching but if I don't like coaching I'm screwed really. I haven't got an awful lot else going on."

Duff has completed his UEFA B-license and in addition to playing for Shamrock Rovers he is also coaching their U15s. That means he's wrestling with a question that confronts every great footballer who becomes a coach: how to deconstruct and explain the skills that came so naturally to him?

"I guess that's probably when I'm at my worst, or any player, any sportsman - when you think about how you're gonna do it, it just doesn't happen. So it's interesting with the U15s - I look at them and I'm like, I don't really know how I've done that. I'm trying to tell kids how I've done something but I don't really know myself. So I'm having to rethink about how I've done things over the years. I'm kinda holding off to do a one-on-one wingers' session with someone, cos I'm like, I'm not really sure how I did it. So I have to take a step back, strip it back, figure out why I did what I was doing."

If you take Duff's word for it, he is currently one of the worst coaches in the world. "Actually, the first session I got given to do with the B license was wingers - attacking play - and I was horrendous. First time I've ever coached, mind, so it was nerve-racking enough, but it was like, a disgraceful session, so bad..."

What actually happened?

"All the FAS lads come out, there's 14, 16 players, and you're just told OK, you're working with the wingers. Improve their wing play. And like, I was just horrendous."

I'm laughing at this image. What went wrong?

"Just the session died a death, and I walked off going, fuck me you're so bad at being a coach. I was just looking at them, I couldn't explain to them. The winger was maybe cutting inside or whatever and he'd maybe give the ball away, and I'm thinking, "what is he doing, like?" but when I actually had to go over there and tell him how to do it, I couldn't help him. So, like I say, it's just stripping it back now. When I'm on the pitch, and it's the same with any player, you're at your best when you don't think."

I say I recently heard Chris Waddle

giving some good insights into how to beat players on Graham Hunter's podcast. The way Duff immediately analyses Waddle's dribbling makes you suspect his evaluation of his own coaching credentials was a bit harsh.

"His dribbling was a one-off. He kind of drags the ball rather than running off his front foot. When you think of most wingers, that's the way they dribble, but not Waddle. He's obviously mastered that when he was a kid, maybe because he wasn't as quick as other players."

"Actually, I've kinda reverted to that now I'm not as quick as I was when I was 18. To be driving with the ball on your front foot you need to be quick. If you look at a lot of the Barcelona players - look at Iniesta - when he dribbles, he doesn't tip it along with the front foot, he more drags the ball, it's beneath him or even behind him. Waddle did that, Zidane as well.

And it's harder for you to get it if you're the defender." "I remember Alan Irvine [the Scottish coach Duff first encountered at Blackburn] showing us that when we were 16. I was like, what are you showing us this for? Now when I look back, they were amazing sessions. Because you don't see many people dribbling like that, off your back foot. Something to maybe pass on to the younger lads at Rovers when I figure out how to tell them what to do."

Just then two lads who have been hovering a few yards away in the hotel bar approach the table. They're about 16 or 17 and they look excited.

"Are you Damien Duff bud?"
"Yeah, you alright?"
"Can I get an autograph off you??"
"Yeah, yeah."
"Are you really Damien Duff??"
They're super-excited now.
"Yeah, you alright?"
"Here, man, you are a legend!"
"Yeah, what's the craic?"
"You are a legend man! Only for you, we have been let down only for you!"
"Ah… for God's sake…"
"No, straight! If you were still out there, we'd be slaughtering every team!"
"Alright."
"Thanks very much bud! Pleasure meeting you!"
"God bless, thanks very much, good luck."
"Such a legend man! Such a legend! Thanks very much bud!"

They go off, delighted with themselves. I ask Duff how that sort of situation makes him feel.

"Well… back in the day I didn't enjoy it. A bit embarrassed or whatever. But I guess you'd be more worried if they weren't coming up, or they were saying you were shite. I'm sure there's a bit inside me… it is nice when people are coming up and saying, 'well done' or 'I like you'. I've had the opposite plenty of times as well, don't worry about that. There's always someone out there, a few haters."

That surprises me. Surely there can't have been too many haters in Ireland?

"Well, in Newcastle I had a few run-ins. Lads following me down the street into restaurants, like. It's character building, that's the way I look at it. Made me a stronger person."

Duff always seemed to me to be acutely uncomfortable with the idea that people might think he had started to think of himself as big-time.

"I guess it's just not in me maybe, the way I was brought up. My Ma and Da, they'd probably give me a clatter, my school friends as well… I was always shy, I'd just play football and go back and wouldn't really say boo to anyone. And it was part of my football education and life education at Blackburn. It was a hard school over there - Kenny Dalglish, Alan Irvine. The minute you stepped out of line or if you even said anything that

was regarded as big-headed or big-time you'd be dropped or mullered, so…"

Did that ever actually happen? "Yeah, once and it wasn't even being big-time! I just asked my landlady if we could get Sky in so we could watch the football. We were missing all the Monday night football on Sky. It had just started and was getting big, and whatever way she's relayed it back to Kenny and Alan Irvine, "Damien Duff is up, kicking up

his shit looking for Sky" - and I actually wasn't. I just said can we get Sky in to watch a bit of footie. So I got called into the office and got fuckin' *stripped*. I still remember that conversation to this day… Little things like that you kind of learn, and that's just how I was brought up."

Was his natural shyness a problem when he first went over to Blackburn?

"Well… when I was 16, even compared to 16-year-old English lads, some of them were full-grown men. They'd be up to all sorts at weekends, they'd be saying what they were doing, and they'd be like - you doing that Duffer? And I'm just like "oh yeah, yeah…" I didn't have a clue what they were on about. I'm sure you know what I mean. But life in football, in the dressing rooms, just hardens you. It'll either make you or break you. I wasn't the most vocal or confident in the beginning, but I had a hunger and desire no-one else had."

"Alan Irvine was one of the best coaches I've ever worked with. He was tough on all of us. That's the way I've always liked it. I don't like arms around the shoulder. I like a kick up the arse, even now. It keeps you on your toes. I don't like to be told if I'm good or I'm this or I'm that, it just makes you lazy. You might take your foot off the gas.

"But everyone's different. I think Shane Long's been getting a bit off Martin O'Neill in the press, recently. Whether that's the right way to go with him, I dunno. I would have thought Shane's more an arm around the shoulder fella. But I dunno. He came on the other night [against Georgia] and did well, so. Everyone's different. I just like a rocket up me hole…"

It's a lesson in why you should never mistake shyness for a

lack of deep confidence. I think Duff prefers criticism to praise because he's good and he knows he is. The ability to take criticism and put it to good use only comes with self-belief. Not everyone has the security of really believing in themselves.

The first time I heard of Damien Duff was during the summer of 1997, when word started to spread about the Ireland underage side that was doing great things in the FIFA World Youth Championships in Malaysia. Brian Kerr's Irish team, with a young Duff to the fore, finished third overall. I wonder if that was important for Duff's confidence at that stage in his career.

"It makes you think you can, I suppose, mix it with the big boys. We played Argentina in the semis, they had Cambiasso, Riquelme, and Aimar in midfield. Even then they were big names. Looking back now, maybe it gives you that bit of belief to kick on. To be honest, at Blackburn there was already a pathway for me, they were lining me up to be in the first team already. But you mention Brian Kerr. He won the 16s and 18s Euros, third in the world in 1997 - for him not to be involved with underage football here is… it's laughable.

Duff describes Kerr as "almost like a second Dad to me when I was starting out," and feels he was harshly dismissed from the senior Ireland job. "We did extremely well under him. It

was the two Israel games. Israel away, they scored in the last minute. I think I hit the bar in the minute after. If we'd won those two games, we would have gone to the Euros and he would have been the next best thing. And I think John [Delaney] came in then and just got rid didn't he? He wanted Stan in. I guess that's football. People want their own people. But to get rid of Brian - he had us at 14th in the world, anyone that came to Lansdowne, they more or less got beat. Sad

BUT YOU MENTION BRIAN KERR. HE WON THE 16S AND 18S EUROS, THIRD IN THE WORLD IN 1997 - FOR HIM NOT TO BE INVOLVED WITH UNDERAGE FOOTBALL HERE IS… IT'S LAUGHABLE…

really. And then, it doesn't help him that he had the senior job to step back down to youth level, but the fact that he's not involved is… crazy. It's laughable. I don't think any words can describe it."

Duff thinks Irish football in general could be doing a better job of tapping into the experience of all those retired players who have represented Ireland.

"I find it sad that there's no ex-players involved with the underage setup here. I don't think there's any, is there? Some lads have done like an ambassador type thing, or appearances. I guess not many live here, and you have to earn your stripes and get your badges. I know there's lads who want to be involved, but… it's a difficult organisation to get into, maybe."

Duff's senior debut for Ireland came in 1998, just after his 19th birthday, but it took him a couple of years to really establish himself in the team. There was a hernia problem, then he briefly became a victim of late-1990s sports science.

"I remember being overweight at the time. It was actually me thinking I was being good. Oh, pasta's good for you, so I'll eat fucking loads of it. I was like a stone overweight. Eventually someone came into the club - what are you doing? Eating two, three bowls of pasta for dinner? You can't do that! Yeah, I was a stone and four, five pounds over. Which meant I couldn't really affect games." There's not a pick on him now. "I'm good like that. You can't eat much as you get older. I'm literally living on salad leaves" at home.

In the summer of 2003, Duff had just completed a brilliant season with Blackburn when Roman Abramovich took over at Chelsea and promptly spent £120 million on 14 new players. The 24-year old Duff became one of the first signings of Chelsea's superpower era.

"I'd nearly joined Liverpool a couple of times, nearly joined Man United, but Blackburn were looking for £17 million. Chelsea just said: here you are. So it was more or less just them then - I had to make a decision. I was so happy at Blackburn, playing so well. Sometimes you see players make these big moves and it doesn't work out. It wasn't anything to do with money, people who know me know I'm not driven by that. I just went down there a couple of times, thought about it for a few days, and eventually I knew, from a football point of view I can't turn this down. The plans they have, the way the club is going. And I was proved right."

"The first couple of weeks there were crazy. You had to pinch yourself. Training with guys like Crespo, Veron, some of the lads who were already there - Marcel Desailly. It was mental. But you can't get carried away by the names. You've gone from playing every week to really fighting for your place. It didn't bother me - it was exciting.

Duff won the Premier League in his second and third seasons at Chelsea. In 2004/5, they won the title with a record 95 points. They had a powerful spine with Terry, Makelele, Lampard and Drogba, but the thing everyone loved about the team was the brilliance

of Duff and Arjen Robben on the wings.

2004/05 was also Jose Mourinho's first year at Chelsea and the wingers in Jose Mourinho teams don't have it easy. Every player is expected to do his defensive duty. Risky dribbling and off-the-cuff individuality is discouraged. Under Mourinho's influence, Duff's game began to evolve. The change was not to everyone's taste. People complained

THE DAY I LEFT HE CALLED ME INTO THE OFFICE. HE GOES: YOU KNOW IF YOU'RE FIT AND YOU'RE PLAYING WELL YOU'LL ALWAYS START IN MY TEAM. AND I WAS JUST LIKE... YEAH.

Mourinho was making him into a boring player. Did they have a point?

"I remember that, lads shouting at me. I remember hearing it a couple of times. At Newcastle say, I wasn't giving the ball away, but if I passed it backwards I'd be fucking slaughtered. That's just the way I was coached, to kill a game. You can look at it in two ways. It makes you a better footballer in one way, but you

kinda lose that other bit, that, I dunno, fearlessness, or the idea that you just get on the ball and do what you want with it. You get fans, like yourself, saying "what's wrong with him?" In one way, I'd totally agree with that side of it. But I still wouldn't change it. Maybe to the fans it's not exciting to watch, but I think it's built me into an all-round better footballer. I'd like to think I can play anywhere on the pitch now.

"The more you're coached, the more it's gonna happen, you're gonna lose that side of you. You can always fight to get it back. But you don't see much of this wing play any more. There's so much coaching. When I was starting it was just like, give Duffer the ball and let him go run at people. But... it's just the way the game's gone. It's all about results, dog-eat-dog, the dark arts of the game. If someone's going by you, you have to take a yellow card or they break and score a goal. Diving. You *have* to dive now. You *have* to win penalties, you *have* to win free kicks." I can remember hearing him talk fairly openly about diving in the past.

"Well, yeah... I've always had probably a little tumble in me locker... if you give me a little nudge. But ... it's an art."

I was behind the goal when he went down to win that penalty against Spain and I tell him now that from my point of view, in real time, his dive was very realistic. He corrects me sharply.

"Oh no - that actually was a penalty." He's serious. Maybe I'll have to look at it again. "Oh no. That one was, yeah. No, no no. That was a penalty."

Duff left Chelsea in 2006 with the first Mourinho era still in full swing. I wondered if he was chafing against the restrictions of playing in a Mourinho team - and maybe also against the personality of Mourinho, whose relationships with players haven't always been stable over the long term. Duff, it turns out, has nothing but respect for his old coach.

"He was amazing. All the dressing room loved him. An amazing coach, which probably a lot of people don't see. They just see this big character, who has all the lads fighting for him, but on the training ground he's amazing. Amazing tactician, amazing sessions every day. For me he's the whole package. I can't speak highly enough of him. I loved him to bits."

I get the impression that if Duff didn't really think this about Mourinho, he wouldn't bother saying it. But if his relationship with the manager was still good, why did he leave?

"Well, towards the end I was in and out of the team. Me being a stubborn Irishman, after three years there - I was just like, ah fuck this, I'm out of here. In hindsight, I should have stayed around and fought for my place - which is what I've always done. I was just getting frustrated that I was missing out minutes and

games in my career that I wasn't going to get back. I love playing football. So I said good luck…" I still don't quite get it. Even if he'd been in and out towards the end, he had been a first-team player for most of his time at Chelsea, including most of the time he had been playing for Mourinho. Had he, for some reason, lost faith that he could regain that status?

"I remember the summer that I left. I knew that when [Mourinho]

was at Porto he was always a fan of the diamond. We had big players in midfield already, and we signed Ballack and then Shevchenko, and we had Drogba. So it looked to me that he wasn't going to play with wingers - definitely not two, maybe one. So I probably didn't back myself enough. And he ended up still playing with wingers and dropping Shevchenko. So I say to any of the kids, just always back yourself and believe in yourself. Maybe I didn't do it there. I said:

I'm off to play football every week. And that doesn't always work out too good either."

Did Mourinho try to persuade him to stay?

"He did. The day I left he called me into the office. He goes: you know if you're fit and you're playing well you'll always start in my team. And I was just like… yeah."

You didn't believe him?

"I do have a stubbornness about me. My wife will tell you, my ma will tell you. I was just like, yeah, my decision's made. I had made my mind up that I was going. Probably if I knew then I was making the wrong decision I'd still go, because I was so stubborn… I still wouldn't change it for the world. I went to Newcastle, three really hard years. The most difficult years of my life, even off the pitch. I couldn't even walk down the road because I'd just get abused. I can laugh about it now, but I honestly couldn't leave my house some days. Small town, massive club, and if the team isn't doing well, which it didn't for really the three years that I was there, all the punters just slaughter you. It was an … interesting time. Hahaha."

The most 'interesting' time of Duff's Ireland career was probably Saipan and its aftermath at the 2002 World Cup. I ask him for the first word that comes into his mind when he thinks of it. There's a long pause. He's obviously considering, and rejecting, several possible words.

"I do laugh," he eventually says. "The amount of times I've regaled the story to people, compared it to things... I was only young. Roy obviously wasn't happy. We were all just laughing about it. But that was just the standards he'd set. The rest of us, we were just like ah, grand, we'll go and have a pint, go have a game of beach football or something. But I guess that's the Irish mentality which pissed him off and does piss him off. Which would piss me off as well now."

If the 36-year-old Duff was back in Keane's position in Saipan, he too might blow his top?

"Yeah. I wouldn't walk though. Obviously. That's next level. But yeah, I'd be fucking livid. It could be a bit loose back in the day at times. The fire engine on the pitch, no balls and kit and all... schoolboy stuff... is that doing a disservice to schoolboy football? We've balls and kit every week with Rovers 15s. I think back and smile and you could call that a great time. It was just one big crazy rollercoaster adventure. It was just a shame we didn't go further. Spain - I know they weren't a superpower at the time. But I remember battering them for the last hour of the game. I remember the possession that night was 52-48

in Ireland's favour." Duff smiles thinly.

"Times have changed."

Another thing that's changed is the relations between the Irish players and media. Remember that one of the things that pissed Keane off in Saipan was that journalists were invited to a

I GUESS THAT'S THE IRISH MENTALITY WHICH PISSED HIM OFF AND DOES PISS HIM OFF. WHICH WOULD PISS ME OFF AS WELL NOW.

barbecue with the players and staff. Thanks in part to the anger and vitriol of the post-Saipan fallout, that barbecue could never happen now.

"We were all kind of one big group back then, then obviously it became more you and us, a bit of friction. But the world is

different now. Back then you'd be going out with reporters and having 20 pints. You do anything now, it's straight on Facebook and Twitter. I don't think it's gonna go back to what it was. "But I don't think results helped either. Steve came in as manager, things dropped off a bit. I don't really get into a lot of arguments, but even I was going over to reporters and having a bite, which doesn't help me. I think back, just bite your tongue. But I was pissed off. People tell me, the people who do the headlines are different from the ones who write the stories? Well, I'd like to get a hold of a couple of them. They screwed me a couple of times.

"Some lads over the years have got personal, some ridiculous articles. It does piss the lads off and it does build barriers. Take the other night, 1-0 against Georgia, I guess not a lot of positives to come out of the performance. I don't read a lot of the press, but I'm sure there's gonna be stuff written... you can't expect lads then to be coming in, hugging and kissing reporters."

Maybe the low point was the aftermath of the 5-2 game in Cyprus in 2006.

"That was a bit distasteful, dropping it down a gear. I think Miss Piggy and the Muppets were there. I was just like... this is fucking nonsense, this lark. I wanted to get out and give them a fucking hiding, like. But you just had to keep the head down. We'd just got a hiding off Cyprus. But teams don't go to Cyprus and win easily. I remember we'd been there and only won 1-0 under Kerrser. Then… OK, a shambles on the night, a lot of mistakes. But ten, twenty years ago, you're expected to win 8-0. Now you're lucky to come out with a result."

I agree that the Muppet thing wasn't great. But neither was losing 5-2 to Cyprus.

"Yeah, I know, yeah."

Still, Duff gets annoyed by people who don't realise how hard it is to get good results in international football.

"Remember when we played Armenia…" Ireland had two narrow wins against Armenia in Euro 2012 qualifying, 1-0 in Yerevan and 2-1 in Dublin.

"You'll get some fans going to that Armenia game - 'Armenia, haven't even heard of them, didn't know they were a country, we'll beat them 5-0'. And ten minutes into the game I was thinking, *these are fucking alright man - these are a good team.* Remember, they beat Slovakia 4-0. The guy that's at Borussia Dortmund now, Mkhitaryan - he was at Shakhtar. I think I'd just played Shakhtar with Fulham, and I was like, watch this geezer, he's a fucking joke like. The fans, there's good and bad, they'll be going to the game thinking 'we'll pump these'. But Armenia are a good team! I'd say they're better than us! Better technically than us. Like, he's a world-beater, that fella. And I remember, amazingly enough, we did beat them. But that was what, four or five years ago? It'd be different now I bet."

Duff's Ireland career came to an

HE'D BE A GOOD FRIEND OF MINE, I LOVE HIM TO PIECES, BECAUSE HE JUST SAYS IT HOW IT IS. WHICH IS AN ADMIRABLE QUALITY. I LOVE HIM, HE'S A HELL OF A GUY.

end at Euro 2012. At first, he was excited to be drawn in a group with Spain, Croatia and Italy.

"Of course we thought we could get through! A million percent. Then, by halfway through the Spain game we were like…. right. This is just damage limitation now. Italy and Spain got to the final, Croatia were a hell

of a good team. It was just the manner of it, I guess, we got pumped off them really."

He won his 100th and final cap against Italy, on a night when Giovanni Trapattoni resisted pressure to change his team and give a game to some of the players who hadn't yet featured in the tournament.

"That's what a lot of managers would have done, but he always stuck by the lads that got him there, I guess, rightly or wrongly. I was dead on me feet not long into the game. I gave Hunty… like if one man deserved an appearance at the Euros it was him. I remember going up to him and giving him a big hug and a kiss afterwards. I said to him, listen, sorry you didn't get on. If there was one man it should have been you. And he broke down in tears. I was like, OK, I wasn't looking for that reaction… but listen. When Hunty first got in the squad I was like, ah, pain in the hole, you're this, you're that, chirping up about me. But now he'd be a good friend of mine, I love him to pieces, because he just says it how it is. Which is an admirable quality. I love him, he's a hell of a guy. Yeah, that was the one thing I remember. Probably the only thing I remember from that 100th cap. It was a bit of a blur. It was how upset he was not to get on. And I was gutted for him as well. Because he's a great lad."

I wonder who Duff's other friends are in football.

"Robbie obviously with the national team. From Blackburn - Jonathan Douglas a bit. Otherwise no-one there. No-one at Newcastle. Sorry - Shay obviously. Stephen Carr. That'd be about it there. Probably in latter years, you start to grow up yourself, you start to make friends. Fulham - some Fulham lads. Bobby Zamora, Brede Hangeland, Aaron Hughes. I had an amazing time there. Proper football team. Nobody came to Craven Cottage and won. But from back in the day, none really. Still in touch with a few people from Melbourne, good people over there. But otherwise you move on, ships in the night. Like, I wouldn't ring any of them really, it'd just be the odd text, a bit of crack and all."

Robbie sent him a "Welcome to Tallaght" message when he joined Rovers. I ask if he's been over to see the Robbie show at LA Galaxy. He hasn't, but he seems to think the chance will be there for a few more years yet. "He runs the place! He'll still be there for another few years.

He's just so clever on the pitch, he could play there till he's 40. Defenders over there can't live with his movement. He could play there into his 40s. He's just so clever around the box. He's still just doing the stuff he was doing on the street really. It wasn't coached into him. He just learned it playing himself."
For a coach, he doesn't sound like the world's biggest fan of coaching.

"Em… Well, not when you talk about this exciting thing, you can't teach someone to be exciting. They have to figure it out for themselves. And then… and then it's up to us coaches to coach it out of them. That's what happens."

Duff has to go to an appointment: his daughter Darcy's third birthday party. "The birthday's tomorrow but it kind of starts today. She has a couple of parties, typical women, so it's the bouncy castle and all…"

As he's leaving I ask how his son, Woody, is getting along. Woody was born with a heart problem that required corrective surgery soon after his birth in 2011. He has since made a full recovery.

"He's grand, yeah. You know, I hate even saying that in the press. When you do something, and they ask you about it… I don't want to bring the story up again. So I hate even seeing it then. Like, the charity thing [Duff's Rovers wages are donated to Heart Children Ireland] wasn't because of him. I just wanted to give it to charity. And it was like, is that because your son - and I was like, well, yeah, it was a hard time, but he's grand, he's flying around. He just has a scar. But he drives me up the wall some days as well."

"He's actually doing martial arts now - mixed martial arts! So I bring him down every Tuesday and Thursday. You have to laugh. I'll have to be the dad going into the ring with the belt."

DUFF CAREER STATS

PERSONAL INFORMATION

NAME: DAMIEN ANTHONY DUFF

DATE OF BIRTH: 2 MARCH 1979 (AGE 36)

PLACE OF BIRTH: BALLYBODEN, DUBLIN

HEIGHT: 1.77 M (5 FT 10 IN)

PLAYING POSITION: WINGER

PLAYING CAREER	PLYD	GLS
REPUBLIC OF IRELAND	100	8
BLACKBURN ROVERS	223	35
CHELSEA	125	19
NEWCASTLE	86	6
FULHAM	173	22
MELBOURNE	15	0
SHAMROCK ROVERS	7	0

CAREER HONOURS

PREMIER LEAGUE	2
LEAGUE CUP	2
COMMUNITY SHIELD	1
INTERTOTO CUP	1

THE DREAM DEBUT

SUPER TERRY MONAGHAN

WEST HAM V GRIMSBY

GO TERRY

TERRY CELEBRATES WILDLY

THE GAFFER

Later

I'M PUTTING YOU ON THE TEAM FOR THE PREMIER GAME THIS WEEKEND

!

THE SUN

THURSDAY

IRISH WONDER KID DOES IT AGAIN

opta terry — Optaterry @ Optaterry

"The lad's done brilliantly" - Chris KAMARA

WEST HAM FIRST SEASON

SO LAD, WHAT YOU UP TO FOR THE SUMMER?

A DO YOU B

GO ON THE IRELAND INTERNATIONAL TRIP TO THE CARIBBEAN FOR YOUR FIRST CAP AGAINST THE CAYMAN ISLANDS

FEIGN INJURY AND GO ON A LADS HOLIDAY TO TENERIFE

GO TO PAGE 51   GO TO PAGE 63

THE GOLDEN
OF SPORTSWRITING

Having been captivated by his radio interviews with Jerry Izenberg over the years, *Eoin McDevitt* travelled to the home of the legendary sportswriter *Jerry Izenberg* in Las Vegas.

The plaque on the living room wall forces me to do a double take. "1997 Pulitzer Prize for Commentary: Jerry Izenberg." My notes had told me the Pulitzer was just about the only award that Izenberg hasn't won, despite being nominated fifteen times. The mystery is solved when we lean in close enough for him to read the punchline, etched in tiny letters: "It don't matter what the committee says, I know more about writin' than any committee." Signed, sealed and delivered by Muhammad Ali. As birthday presents go, you'd have to be reasonably happy with that one.

Jerry Izenberg is a giant of sportswriting. His career spans more than sixty years, most of them spent working as a columnist with the New Jersey-based *Star-Ledger* newspaper. In that time, he has covered every single Super Bowl, found himself in the company of some of the world's greatest heads of state and some of its most evil dictators, and befriended the most famous athlete of the twentieth century.

I wasn't totally sure what to expect when I travelled to Nevada to meet Jerry face-to-face earlier this year. I've interviewed him a number of times in the past but there's a hell of a difference between a twenty-minute chat on the phone and rocking up to a person's house to badger him for as many hours as good manners will allow.

It's reasonable to suggest he has something of a gruff exterior and

the taxi driver who picked me up at Las Vegas Airport did look a little ashen-faced after a call to Izenberg failed to strengthen the man's shaky sense of direction. A second cabbie eventually took over from our stricken friend and proceeded to whisk me away from the delights of the Strip, out through the desert, and up towards the mountains of nearby Henderson, where Jerry was waiting with a warm welcome, a cup of coffee, and a strongly-held opinion that all taxi drivers really should be armed with GPS.

Jerry's wife had just gone to catch a flight, leaving the two of us alone in their beautiful one-storey home...

ERA

The walls are alive with photographs and memorabilia, and as we stroll around, it feels like I'm getting a guided tour through the social history of American sport by a man who has seen it all. "That [photo], I got my left hand on Ali's jaw. I'm teaching him a lesson, he got a little outta line... Joe Frazier and me in Vegas... this is Larry Doby, first black man to hit a home run in a World Series, and a pitcher named Steve Gromek; the first time I'm sure a black man and a white man hugging was on the front page of an American newspaper."

We sit down to chat amidst the organised chaos of Jerry's workspace. I find a spot to rest my laptop beside a mug emblazoned with the words: 'Trust me... I'm a reporter'. Behind us, Jerry's own bibliography takes its place among an impressive book collection. In the distance, out past the pool at the back of the house, the most decadent city in the world shimmers and glistens, but Vegas may as well be a million miles from this oasis of calm. When he considers the qualities that best define Ali, his friend, he's keen to stress one characteristic

above all others. "Nobody that I know, maybe Pacquiao in some ways, feels for young people and old people the way Muhammad did." He recalls a night when the two of them watched a tug-at-the-heartstrings news story about a Jewish old age home in the Bronx that was on the verge of shutting

its doors for the winter. "So Ali said 'Let's go.'" With that, they're off to the Bronx where the boxer meets the rabbi in charge and has a cheque made out for whatever amount is needed to save the place. "Typical Ali, he's done the whole thing outta the goodness of his heart but also, he can't miss

his exit line. So he gets up, it's like Cecil B. DeMille is directing this thing. He turns, he takes four steps, he stops. He turns [back]... his face is stage right and he says: 'Now get the money next year from the Jews 'cos they got a lotta money.'"

Jerry fought Ali's corner during the Vietnam War, when the heavyweight champ was stripped of his title after he refused to be drafted into the U.S. Army. This support was based not on their friendship, according to Izenberg, but on his belief in the U.S. Constitution. He got down to business, wrote up the first of his columns on the subject "and then it all started." Bomb threats to the office, dog faeces in the post, a sledgehammer attack on his car. When police asked Jerry if he knew of anybody who didn't like him, he replied: "Officer, it's like Sunday morning at the delicatessen, take a number and you'll be served eventually." If it was a scary time for Izenberg, he doesn't sound like he regrets a single word that he wrote.

He delivers these stories in a deep, gravelly, from-the-back-of-

JERRY IZENBERG TIMELINE

1930: Born in Newark, New Jersey

1951: Begins his journalism career as copy boy with the *Newark Star-Ledger*.

1964: Witnesses Muhammad Ali, then Cassius Clay, take the world heavyweight championship from Sonny Liston

1967: Covers Super Bowl I, the first of forty-nine consecutive Super Bowls he has attended

1969: Writes a piece called 'Liberty and Justice for All', defending Ali's right to refuse to be drafted into the U.S. Army during the Vietnam War

the-throat voice, while somehow managing to infuse them with a curious softness. Side-splitting laughter is not his thing but, behind the grey goatee beard, an amused smile regularly breaks out and lights up an otherwise inscrutable face. He's happy to poke fun at himself when it comes to such issues as his lack of height, stopping at a photograph of a determined-looking eight-year-old baseball player and exclaiming: "Physically, as a specimen, it's been downhill for me ever since then."

Izenberg was born in Newark, New Jersey on September 10th, 1930 ("the worst year of the Great Depression"). He traces his love of sport back to the day his father bought him his first baseball glove. Harry Izenberg had forged a professional career in the minor leagues, having arrived in the country as a young boy in the late 1800s. "He was born in a slice of Eastern Europe. On Tuesdays it was Russia, on Thursdays it was Poland, on Tuesdays Russia again, but the Jews were getting the crap kicked out of them no matter what it was."

Jerry's life in journalism began in 1951 when he landed a job as a copy boy at his local paper, *The Star-Ledger.* "In those days they didn't have tubes or anything; it was hot type, you'd take the copy they would write, you'd run up another floor, you'd hand it to the guy... Within a week they said 'Hey

JERRY FOUGHT ALI'S CORNER DURING THE VIETNAM WAR, WHEN THE HEAVYWEIGHT CHAMP WAS STRIPPED OF HIS TITLE AFTER HE REFUSED TO BE DRAFTED INTO THE U.S. ARMY.

kid, you're gonna start writing things.'"

By the time of his first trip to baseball's spring training in Arizona, during a stint with the *New York Herald Tribune,* the cub reporter was confident he had the writing game sussed. Cranking out

what he describes as "pure poetry," he was shocked to be called back to the office by his editor and mentor Stanley Woodward. "I get back, I sit down with him and he said 'Who's gonna play second base for the Giants?' And I said 'That's a good question, you know there's five guys, they're lined up, I'm really not sure.' He said 'Lemme tell ya something young man, I don't give a shit about the painted desert that you're writing about, I don't give a damn about the fact that the Lost Dutchman's Mine is thirteen miles from where the Houston Astros are training, I wanna know who's gonna play second base for the Giants! Now you go sit down at that desk and you figure it out.' And he left me there for three months."

Mercifully, Jerry escaped from the shackles of the office and set about experiencing some of the biggest days sport had to offer. He's one of only two daily columnists who can boast a perfect Super Bowl attendance record and he plans to make it fifty-in-a-row in 2016. He remembers the inaugural staging of the event in 1967 as a

1971:	**1974:**	**1989:**	**2000:**	**2000:**	**2007:**
Produces the Emmy-nominated TV documentary 'A Man Named Lombardi'	Travels to Zaire to report on the Rumble in the Jungle	Writes an eyewitness account of the Loma Prieta earthquake that struck San Francisco minutes before the start of a World Series baseball game between the Giants and the Oakland A's	Wins the Associated Press Red Smith Award for major contributions to sports journalism	Inducted into the National Sportscasters and Sportswriters Hall of Fame	Retires from full-time duty with *The Star-Ledger* but continues to contribute regularly to the newspaper, while also devoting time to a number of book projects

time before the "NFL Gestapo" regulated media access to the players. "There's no way you could do it [now] unless you kidnapped a player. I'm actually having breakfast, two days before the first Super Bowl, with a guy named E.J. Holub whose nickname is 'The Beast'... I'm asking him about nerves... and he reaches across the table, puts his hands out, palms up, he says 'Feel my hands.' They're wet. He's sweating. And I said, schmuck I was, I said 'Is this because now you could maybe beat these guys and you could show the world you belong?' He looked at me like I just landed from Mars. He said 'Do you realise if we win this game I get fifteen thousand dollars and my wife has already spent it?!'"

You may have guessed by now that Jerry Izenberg can spin a hell of a yarn. Or, as he puts it himself, "You always get a double story from me and I can't help it. When you get old, you talk." Just because an anecdote begins with eight-year-old Jerry cheering the radio commentary of Joe Louis avenging his defeat to Max Schmeling, doesn't mean it can't end at Sonny Liston's funeral more than thirty years later. The best course of action is to sit back, buckle up and go along for the ride.

The only subject he's reluctant to talk about is his time in service during the Korean War. That period in his life does, however, provide the backdrop to a poignant scene between father and son, a scene I stumble across when I point to one of the framed columns dotted around the place. The focal point of the column is a conversation Jerry had with his dad when he got his orders to go

to Korea. Harry Izenberg, who was wounded in World War I, urges his son to take care of himself and, for many years, that's how the story ended.

Recently, Jerry added another layer to the article "because I'd left it out for too long." His voice is heavy with emotion as he recites the updated ending from memory: "There was a day when both my father and I knew he was

dying and he said to me 'Go up in my closet, I want to show you something.' Looked in the closet, he said 'Whaddya see?' I said 'Well, sport jacket, a couple of pairs of pants, two shirts, pair of shoes.' He said 'OK,' he came over to me, he said 'Now you know. I have nothing to leave you except my good name.' Then he put his arm around my shoulders, and he smiled at me and he said: 'Don't screw it up.'"

As my visit creeps into its third hour, it dawns on me that I should probably let the man get back to work. In his mid-80s now, Izenberg still contributes to The Star-Ledger, and as recently as last year released his latest book, a biography of the longtime NFL Commissioner Pete Rozelle.

When he reflects on the legacy he'd like to leave, he's not too concerned with the awards he's received, not even the Muhammad Ali-designed Pulitzer. Instead, he reminds me of something he said to me during the first ever interview I did with him: "When this is over," he's speaking slowly and deliberately now, "I hope that [my readers] can say: 'Well, he's done now but he tried to give us the best he had and you know? It really was the best.' If I can believe they will think that, what prize can equal that?"

IZENBERG, ALI AND FRANK SINATRA'S BULLSHIT

October 1st 1980. Caesars Palace, Las Vegas. The night before Muhammad Ali v Larry Holmes.

He [Ali] comes to my room and he says 'You don't think I can win this fight, do ya?' I said 'I'm not gonna lie to you champ, I don't think you should be in this fight and no, I don't think you can win it.' He rips his shirt off: 'What do you think now?' It was like a ghostly presence, he looked exactly like he looked the night he fought Liston, he lost all the weight, and I said to him 'You know, you coulda done that at the European Health Spa.' I had no way of knowing they had him on diuretics, he could hardly lift his arms.

So we go to the fight and it's horrible. I mean it is horrible. I don't care what people say and I've seen the film a couple of times and they're seein' things I can't see, I never saw him throw a punch all night long. I think they stopped it in the ninth, somewheres around then. I jump up, like, two rounds earlier and I yell at [referee] Richard Steele: 'Richard, stop the f'in' fight! You're gonna get this man killed!' And I look around and realise what I've done, it's the most unprofessional act of my entire career, I sat down and I was really embarrassed.

"HE DIDN'T SAY ANYTHING ABOUT WINNING OR LOSING, HE SAID: 'I BET ON THE MAN WHO GAVE ME DIGNITY.' THAT'S REALLY THE WAY TO REMEMBER MUHAMMAD ALI."

Fight stops, okay, Sinatra's being Sinatra, he's in the showroom that night and he's saying (Jerry puts on overly dramatic voice): 'I just came from the room of a wonderful, great man,' because he wants you to know that he saw Ali after the fight. And I was standing in the back of this room, I said 'This is bullshit,' I walk out, and then I'm gambling a little bit, I'm walkin' around and I just felt it was so unsatisfying because the guy [Ali], he pissed on his own dignity, nobody did it for him, alright?

I walk into the men's room, three o'clock in the morning. There's an old gentleman there, black fella, handing out towels. I said 'Sir, you mind if I ask you a question?' He said 'No, go ahead.' I said 'Did you bet on this fight?' He said 'Yes I did.' I said 'Who did you bet on?' He looked at me like I was a Martian or something. He said 'I bet on the man who gave me dignity.'

All the things I thought for all these years, that really summed it up; 'I bet on the man who gave me dignity.' He didn't say 'I knew he would win' or 'I hoped he would [win].' He didn't say anything about winning or losing, he said: 'I bet on the man who gave me dignity.' That's really the way to remember Muhammad Ali.

JERRY IZENBERG CAREER IN NUMBERS

15
Pulitzer Prize nominations

49
Consecutive Super Bowls attended

07
Knockdowns suffered by Floyd Patterson at the hands of Ingemar Johansson in 1959, the first of many heavyweight title fights that Jerry has covered

65
Dollars - Jerry's weekly wage in the 1950s for writing, editing, printing and delivering a small local newspaper

01
Emmy-nominated TV documentary

1000+
Letters of complaint received by Izenberg, attacking him for defending Muhammad Ali's right to refuse to be drafted into the U.S. Army during the Vietnam War

02
Career landmarks in the year 2000: Inducted into the National Sportscasters and Sportswriters Hall of Fame and given the Red Smith Award for major contributions to sports journalism by The Associated Press

64
Years as an active sportswriter (and counting...)

SECTION 2

SECRET DESIRES. FORBIDDEN MAGIC. INTRIGUING MYSTERY. LIMITLESS PASSION. THIS...IS ABBOTSTOWN.

BY DAVID SQUIRES

PLEASE TURN OVER ▶

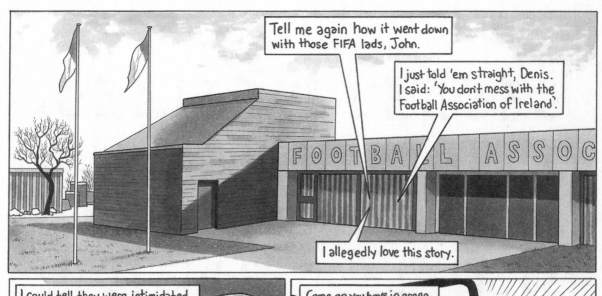

Tell me again how it went down with those FIFA lads, John.

I just told 'em straight, Denis. I said: 'You don't mess with the Football Association of Ireland'.

I allegedly love this story.

I could tell they were intimidated by the way they just shrugged, like they were hiding their fear with complete indifference. So I showed them a YouTube video of my legion of fans, just to force the point home.

Redacted.

Come on you boys in green, come on you boys in green—

Yeaarghh!

Shh! Shh! Shh! Shh! Shhhhh!

Hahahahahahaha hahahahaha ha hahahahaha ha.

And that's when they gave me five million euros to get out of their office. They were playing Jenga with a huge pile of notes, so they just skimmed a few blocks off the top.

And what did the press say?

They thought it was grand!

Until the rest of the world found out.

40

$INCERITY

SPORTS STARS' SECRET SAUCE

Words: Simon Hick

'I want to find out what your feelings are, and did you learn anything' - Earl Woods, from beyond the grave.

Neymar Sr is on the phone, asking if everything's ok for his football superstar son over in Europe. He is wise and supportive, in a poetic kind of way - "Today is another important day in our lives. Today, run like it is the last day of your life. Run like you're a crazy man chasing happiness. Run for your family and your friends. Today be happy. Enjoy football!"

This earnest advice on family and friends and happiness is one part of an elaborate *Beats By Dre* TV advert broadcast last year that also features cameos by Serena Williams, Luis Suarez, Robin Van Persie, Rio Ferdinand, Mario Gotze, and, naturally, Nicki Minaj. Neymar Jr, however, is the undisputed star.

He pops on his headphones, winks at the fans, makes the peace sign to the paparazzi, puts on his shin guards, and stares with intent as he walks out the tunnel. His father's voice emerges from the ether - "Put God's army in front of you. Wear God's armour, from the helmet to the sandals. Go with God. God Bless you. I love you".

The ad is heaving with celebs, flesh, and references to God - the Holy Trinity of marketing - but more than anything else, it has heart; Disney movie levels of heart, all squeezed into a slick looking five minute montage.

It's just one example of a new style of sports marketing that can best be described as 'sincerity sells'. Sports stars, it seems, have a new message to send to their followers: they're good people, people with roots and family connections and faith and loyalty and doubts and dilemmas...

and the best way for them to express these complex human emotions is through the medium of heavy-handed television adverts. Sincerity is the new sex, the elixir of truth.

The first, and probably most famous, mainstream ad of this genre was on the eve of Tiger Woods' Masters comeback in 2010. Tiger stares down the camera lens, unblinking, with just a hint of emotion in his eyes, as his father Earl talks to him from beyond the grave.

"Tiger, I am more prone to be inquisitive. To promote discussion. I want to find out what your thinking was. I want to find out what your feelings are. Did you learn anything?"

The words don't really mean anything, especially as the audio is spliced together from something Earl said in a 2004 documentary when asked to compare himself and his wife Kultida. Nike's objective at the time was to hint at Tiger's inner turmoil, his depth, and to remind you he is not a machine, just another flawed human trying his best to make sense of this crazy world.

Lebron James has since made this sincerity angle the cornerstone of his whole corporate image, particularly during the much-documented return to his home town team the Cleveland Cavaliers. He is the man who wants to save

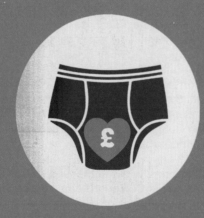

a city from economic ruin by shooting three pointers, and by making television commercials that show just how much he means it.

Both his Nike and his Beats ads feature imagined scenes from his childhood. Lebron's mother crops up a lot, holding his hand, picking him up, looking earnestly into his eyes. LeBron and Neymar and Tiger are all clearly comfortable including their families. They grew up shilling for all they were worth, and if they

have to bring their parents into the marketing mix, so be it.
Bastian Schweinsteiger is a more surprising addition to the *Beats By Dre* sports portfolio. Schweinsteiger was Mr Bayern Munich, a Bavarian born and bred. 17 years at the club, 8 Bundesliga titles, a Champions League medal, total commitment, no off-field issues, a one club man. His move to Manchester United was a surprise because it was hard to associate him with any other club.

In the opening scene of his commercial he's packing up his stuff and leaving his beloved Munich. This, the *Beats By Dre* people want us to know, is not a decision he's taken lightly. He hops into a taxi for the airport, stares wistfully out the window of the car and as his head turns it reveals his headphone brand of choice when making life-altering decisions. Schweinsteiger is taking the high moral ground on club loyalty, and then parlaying that loyalty into further profits. Even Krusty the Klown might have wrestled with that one.

Bling headphones have now become an established symbol of the footballer/NBA/NFL star way of life, a symbol of the money

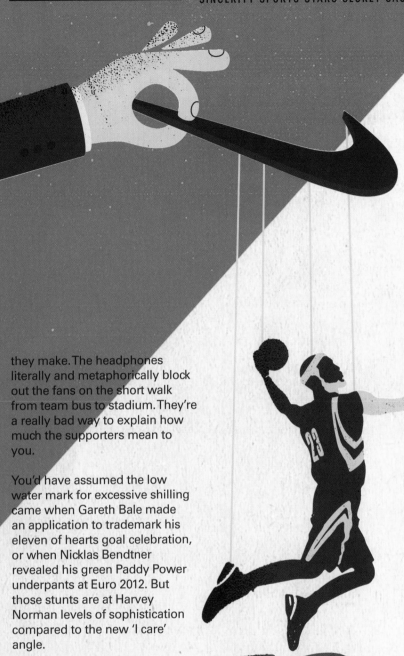

they make. The headphones literally and metaphorically block out the fans on the short walk from team bus to stadium. They're a really bad way to explain how much the supporters mean to you.

You'd have assumed the low water mark for excessive shilling came when Gareth Bale made an application to trademark his eleven of hearts goal celebration, or when Nicklas Bendtner revealed his green Paddy Power underpants at Euro 2012. But those stunts are at Harvey Norman levels of sophistication compared to the new 'I care' angle.

Shilling is a significant part of the job for a professional sports person, but fake sincerity is a new departure. There must be better ways of making money than using your dead father's voice in an ad for sports apparel, and the question is, does it even work?

The fact is sports fans, in general, hate underhandedness. It lasts longer in the memory than medals or cups, and it cuts deeper. Ask for an opinion on Thierry Henry or Tom Brady and you're more likely to hear about the moments they cheated than

you are about the moments of greatness.

What fans are arguably looking for above all else in sport, is sincerity. Sport is at the earnest end of the entertainment spectrum. That's why there are now cameras in the changing rooms before games, player-cams, mic'd up players, in game interviews with coaches and behind the scenes documentaries; because in those moments you might get a glimpse of Paul O'Connell roaring at his teammates or post-fight tears of joy from Katie Taylor.

The trade-off for Tiger and the rest is they lose their moral authority. He probably doesn't care but Neymar's 'look at me' 100% Jesus pose at the end of the Champions League final, for example, has to be viewed with a critical eye in light of his other endorsements. Does he want us to know he loves Jesus, or is an association with Jesus a profitable image for a Brazilian footballer to project.

People buy these products because of the connection with talent and superstardom. Fake sincerity wasn't supposed to be part of the deal.

LEBRON JAMES HAS SINCE MADE THIS SINCERITY ANGLE THE CORNERSTONE OF HIS WHOLE CORPORATE IMAGE

YOU ARE THE JU
YOU make the HARD call:

1.

2.

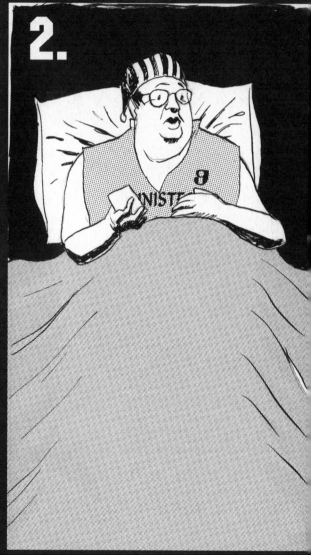

You are 15 minutes away from your first championship game of the year. Your 37-year-old corner-back has opened up his gear bag and instead of boots, he has brought two 1KG bags of wholemeal flour. Can he still play in the match?

Two of your best players are minors on the county panel. Thanks to the young men, you hold an important lead in a local derby match. They have kicked five superb points each and are receiving little help from your other, weaker players. However, they appear to be ignoring all your tactical instructions from the sideline. All is going well on the scoreboard as you approach half-time, do you allow the situation to continue?

ANSWERS

Ans: No, you MUST save face down the pub, your authority cannot be questioned. At half-time, warn the 17 year-olds that they are in danger of "getting too big for their boots" in front of the entire dressing room. Mention that you would have played for the county yourself were it not for injury. Threaten a substitution if they continue to ignore you and shout that you've "plenty of lads ready to come in" (even though you've one sub – an 18 stone man called 'Tiny' who is wearing jeans).

Ans: Yes, let your corner-back to check his car for boots, shoes or runners. Force him to wear his good Dubarry slip-ons or simply remove the boots from your weakest substitute and give to the player. Confiscate flour as punishment.

3.

It's the eve of a big championship match. You receive a text informing you that your captain and star midfielder has been spotted in *Spice* nightclub drinking aftershock. Do you still play him in tomorrow's showdown?

4.

You are picking your team for the first game of the year. In every training session so far this season you have promised that the players who go training will be the players that are picked. However, four of your best players have not been to a single training session, do you pick them?

Ans: Of course: do back to sleep and ignore text. Drive your van to player's house early in the morning to pick him up. Avoid disciplinary action in case he decides not to play anymore.

Ans: Yes. You must get the victory. Make sure to give impassioned pre-match speech warning these four players about their future conduct. Inform them of "how lucky they are" to be getting picked considering the "strong performances in training" of the substitutes. This will make your useless players feel somewhat better about themselves. WARNING: Do NOT then request one of the useless players to act as umpire for the game.

THE TEAM CHOOSES YOU

Words: US Murph

OUR DEAR FRIEND BRIAN MURPHY, CO-PRESENTER OF THE MURPH AND MAC SHOW ON KNBR RADIO IN SAN FRANCISCO, SPENT AN IDYLLIC YEAR IN DUBLIN AS A YOUNG MAN IN 1992. HERE HE REMINISCES ON THAT SUMMER — WORKING AS A BARMAN, SUPPORTING CLARE, AND LONG, BEFORE HE BECAME US MURPH, GETTING A NICKNAME FOR HIMSELF.

In sports, sometimes you get to choose your favorite team. When it came to Clare GAA, it chose me.

As many of you devoted Second Captains listeners know, I spent most of 1992 living in Phibsboro, working a menial job at O'Donoghue's on Merrion Row, and soaking up more craic than a was legal or recommended.

My patron saint in Ireland was a Clare man. We'll call him Brian C., so you all don't hunt him down and ask for his autograph while he tutors the junior hurlers of the Banner County in his middle-aged years.

Brian C. housed me when I disembarked from the Holyhead ferry on a drizzly March night. Brian C. introduced me to my roommates, two Limerick lads. Brian C. also made sure I learned the unwritten rules of Dublin life for a pack of pals in their early 20s: 1. Always be ready to buy your round; 2. A pint of plain is your only man.

Life lessons, sports fans.

I was learning the Dublin lifestyle quickly. Well, not that quickly. Drop a Northern California kid who is used to laid-back surfers using the word "dude" into a pub where Northside Dubliner bartenders use the word "cunt" just as frequently, and there's bound to be some cognitive dissonance. One time, Nicky, our bruising bouncer at O'Donoghue's, laughed at a joke I made while we enjoyed a post-midnight, post-work pint. He tilted his head toward me and said to Pat, another bartender: "'E's a gas cunt, in't he?"

I think it was a compliment.

That didn't stop Nicky from slapping me with my chop-busting nickname: "Woody". Trying to interpret O'Donoghue's bartenders shouting instructions at me over a packed bar, with their Dublin accents thicker than the low-hanging cigarette smoke, my expressions were so frequently blank and befuddled that Nicky finally snapped one day. He shouted over the din and the live music, when I failed to comprehend yet another incomprehensible work order: "You're a thick cunt! Like 'Woody' from the TV!"

He was talking about Cheers.

I don't think it was a compliment, but it was funny.

And that's most what I learned. How funny the Irish were, and how creative the Irish were with their humor, particularly with song. One day, Ireland - then in its heyday under Jack Charlton - beat Switzerland in a friendly, 2-1. I know this because that night at the bar, a man stood up and sang, to the tune of Blue Moon: "Two-onnne …. we beat the Swiss, two-one … we beat the Swiss, two-one."

The smallest little detail, but it made my night.

I later attended a US-Ireland

friendly at old Lansdowne Road. When I cheered for a positive play by the Americans, an Irishman shouted at me: "Sit down! Ye may have won the fucking Gulf War, but you're not winning anything

AND THAT'S MOST WHAT I LEARNED. HOW FUNNY THE IRISH WERE, AND HOW CREATIVE THE IRISH WERE WITH THEIR HUMOR, PARTICULARLY WITH SONG.

today." Topical humor, even.

Anyway, back to Clare and the summer of 1992. One night in the spring, I was with my Clare buddy Brian C. at O'Donoghue's, and we ran into a mate of his. They exchanged pleasantries, and

when the pal walked away, Brian C. said to me: "He's on Clare's Gaelic Football team."

"Whoa!" I said, earnestly. "That's pretty cool."

"They haven't won a Munster title since 1917," Brian C. said, taking a long drag on his fag. "It's not that cool."

1917! Even 'Woody' could understand that with a drought like that, Clare GAA — caught in the crossfire of the Munster heavyweights Kerry and Cork — were a little like the Chicago Cubs of Ireland. Great passion, great fan base. Results? Not so much.

That summer, Neil Diamond played a string of sold-out gigs at Croke Park. Someone asked Brian C. one night at the bar: "What's the difference between Neil Diamond and Clare GAA? Neil Diamond's played Croke Park."
Same stuff happens to Cubs fans in America.

But spring turned to summer and Clare football somehow, some way stayed alive. And then on the magical day of July 19, 1992, at the Gaelic Grounds in Limerick, Clare did it. The Banner trumped The Kingdom. Clare beat Kerry. Munster champions. Shock? Only one of the biggest upsets in recent GAA history, right? You'd have thought U2 announced they were playing a live show in The Burren. (Yes, kids, in 1992, U2 was still on the cool side of the street. Barely, but still.)

I happened to have stayed the night out in Doolin the night before and woke up to streets covered in chalk writing, "WELL DONE CLARE!' and 'COME ON THE BANNER!' and 'UP THE BANNER!' and the names of players scribbled on the pavement. A guy could easily become a bandwagon Clare fan. That guy would be me.

And oh, the look in Brian C.'s eyes. Clare, his beloved home land, where his father raised his clan on the Windswept Hill of Tulla, were the best in Munster. Better yet, they were coming to Croke Park for the first time in 75 years. Even better yet, the semifinal against Dublin wouldn't be until August 23. That meant a month of strutting and wild anticipation.

I look back on those days now as the sweetest of days, overflowing with our carefree youth, the long light of summer, another round on the way, Clare on their way to Croke Park.

The Saturday night before the match was the definition of anticipatory adrenaline. The train up from Clare was laughingly dubbed 'The Culchie Express' — and Clare fans spilled out apologizing for nothing. Brian

I LOOK BACK ON THOSE DAYS NOW AS THE SWEETEST OF DAYS, OVERFLOWING WITH OUR CAREFREE YOUTH, THE LONG LIGHT OF SUMMER, ANOTHER ROUND ON THE WAY, CLARE ON THEIR WAY TO CROKE PARK.

C.'s buddy, Keith, stumbled into the bar a bit of a mess — ripped jeans, dirty shirt, ragamuffin jacket with a stain on it. Mike K. sized him up and roared, "What are ye, BOASTING that you're in from Clare?"

That night, Clare folk doubled down on the culture war with mighty Dublin, singing to the tune of Camptown Races: "Molly Malone was born in Clare/Doo dah/Doo dah…" The Dublin fans could only laugh and raise a glass, and shout back, "Fuck the Shannon Stopover!" Topical airport humor. The craic, she was mighty.

The big day arrived, and I may as well have been Biddy Early's long lost son. We headed to the pub early, not content to allow traditional Sunday hours stop us. "Let us innnn/Let us innnn/Olé, olé, olé" went the chant outside the pub window near Croke Park. When Keith arrived, the song went up again: "Spot the culchie/spot the culchie/Olé, olé, olé…"

More pints, more song. And then a funny thing happened.

All the frivolity, all the jokes, it all dissipated about a half-hour before the match, when it was time for us to enter Croke Park. The boys turned quieter, a wonderful combination of nerves and pride and stomach-churning awe. One-liners gave way to silence as we shuffled into the historic old building. The looks in their eyes changed. And when the saffron yellow and blue jerseys stormed out of the locker room, an unforgettable tableau against the natural green pitch of Croke Park, and the Clare flags waved back and forth in the crowd, well...yeah. You can imagine.

The game itself is a blur. The national anthem, I recall, was hair-raising. Clare played well. Vinny Murphy and Dublin played

a little better. Dublin won. Brian C. and I eventually, after the pubs and the recaps and songs, walked a long way home in the dark, in satisfied silence.

Three years later, everything changed for Clare when their hurling dynasty launched. But on

that August day in 1992, Clare played Croke Park. Neil Diamond, eat your heart out.

Listen to Brian Murphy on The Irish Times Second Captains Podcast every Thursday.

IRELAND'S HERO

Eire Eire Eire

TERRY SCORES A LATE EQUALISER

GOAL

AND CELEBRATES WITH ROBBIE KEANE

DELANEY CELEBRATES WITH JOYOUS SHIFT

...DUNPHY HAS HIS SAY...! HE'S A STREET FOOTBALLER BABY

A DO YOU B

KNUCKLE DOWN FOR ANOTHER SEASON AT WEST HAM

IMMEDIATELY PUSH FOR A BIG MONEY MOVE TO EVERTON

GO TO PAGE 99   GO TO PAGE 93

KEN EARLY:
The Marseille Years

SWORN TO SECRECY BY CHRIS WADDLE IN 1989, KEN EARLY'S CONTROVERSIAL TIME AS A PROFESSIONAL FOOTBALLER HAS REMAINED SHROUDED IN MYSTERY. IN THESE EXCLUSIVE EXTRACTS FROM HIS FORTHCOMING WARTS-AND-ALL AUTOBIOGRAPHY, 'EARLY TO BED, EARLY SURPRISE', KEN EARLY FINALLY REVEALS THE SHOCKING TRUTH ABOUT HIS TIME AT MARSEILLE - HIS GAMBLING PROBLEMS, HIS SEXY LIFESTYLE AND HIS FEUD WITH BASILE BOLI.

EXTRAIT NUMÉRO UN: THE EARLY YEARS

I first came to prominence in the Dublin District Schoolboys League. The exact goal to games ratio in my time as a junior footballer is of no importance (93 goals in just 32 and a half league games). What remains seared onto the brain of those who played with or against me is the 'sneer of cold command' (Keats, Ozymandias) with which I dominated those games. Aloof, professorial, utterly dominant – I was a phenomenon. The people saw no joy in my play but I was exploring the outer reaches of my ability, plumbing the depths of the Mariana Trench that was my God-given talent, and I saw it as a deeply serious responsibility. I knew that some of the big English clubs were interested in

me, but one day we were playing Cherry Orchard, and there was a Gauloises-smoking, Panama-hat-wearing man standing off to the side, watching me with a gimlet eye. He was Pierre De Beaumarchais, part-time actor and Marseille scout.

After the game he came to me and asked to speak to my mother. He seemed like a bit of a horny old goat so I gave him my dad's number instead, and a couple of days later he called out to the house. He spoke at length to my parents, who had some concerns. Would my burgeoning love for poetry be hot-housed and nurtured? Was there a thriving arts scene that I could plug into on my arrival? They also wanted

to know what dialects of French were spoken in the dressingroom (I had been taught French in the Parisian style, but I had also had some experience of the Toulousain and Bretagne dialects during my travels alone through the country as a 13-year-old).

Having been reassured on all counts by Pierre, they came to me with their thoughts. On the whole they thought that Marseille was a good spiritual fit for me. A shared love of French naval history had long been the only thing keeping my family together, and here was a chance to reinforce that bond by moving to one of the great Mediterranean sea-ports. I would depart with the next full tide.

EXTRAIT NUMÉRO DEUX:
MY BITTER RIVALRY WITH BOLI

The feud between Basile Boli and I had its roots in a dinner party I threw in late 1990. Present at the soiree were – philosopher Jacques Derrida, actress Emmanuelle Beart, a pornographer called Ernest, and Jean Pierre Papin. JPP (as I liked to call him) and I were grilling Jacques over the fatuousness of his latest treatise *Force of Law,* when in marched Boli and demanded to see my pet ferret, Marine. Boli was consumed with grief at the death of his own ferret (also called Basile Boli, bizarrely), and became convinced that Marine was in fact Basile Boli.

After the initial shock subsided, I was able to point to the unique colouring, and indeed perfectly timid disposition of Marine, but Boli (the human Basile Boli) was not for turning.

Papin tried to act as intermediary, but he had only a basic knowledge of the ferret world, and only succeeded in exacerbating the situation. Now the first rule of football is that you leave personal issues at the door when you go to training every morning, but Boli was incapable of acting like a professional.

The relationship turned poisonous. My success the previous season, my new clothing line, and my rapacious appetite for women had split the dressing-room. Who was this young guttersnipe? Boli had taken agin me, in the parlance of the snooker hall, and I had made a powerful enemy...

EXTRAIT NUMÉRO TROIS: TURTLE-NECK EVENINGS

The year was 1989 and the city of Marseille was like a magnificent open goal, waiting for me to shoot my football into! My opening game hat-trick against Rennes ensured that my name was on the guest-list at all the best parties, and I was intent on sampling all of the delights available to me.

I became acutely aware of how important it was to project the right image. And so I quickly developed a taste for all the finer

things in life – slip-on shoes, turtle-neck sweaters, and double-breasted suits. There's no doubt about it, I was a thrusting young blade on the Marseille singles scene.

But old habits die hard, and my fascination with the seedy underbelly of the city was bound to get me into trouble. In the apartment below mine, there lived a 68-year-old mother of three... let's call her Mama Isobel. She was one of the main figures in a ruthless underground bridge game, in whose fiendish bosom I admit I found solace from time to time.

I had run up debts of 150 francs or more inside a few months and she warned me that she knew some people who would make life very uncomfortable for me. Given that most of my 100,000 francs-a-week wages went on slip-ons, this was a real problem for me.

I rang Monsieur Tapie, the now-disgraced Marseille chairman, with my problem. He gave it to me straight. He would resolve my debt to Mama Isobel, but only if I co-operated in match fixing. And that was it. With that conversation, I was inside the biggest, most-secretive match-fixing ring in French football history. I knew things that only I, my team-mates, Monsieur Tapie, Monsieur Tapie's hair-dresser, every passenger on the No. 39 bus that I was traveling on at the time, and just a few thousand others were aware of.

Our success was a façade.

EXTRAIT NUMÉRO QUATRE: WADDLE AND ME

The idea is out there that Chris Waddle chased me from Marseille. Nothing could be further from the truth. Sure, he plotted behind my back to get me out of the team, put a contract out on my life, ostracized me from the pottery classes in his house which were a key part of our team-building process, and publicly criticised my play, but I consider Chris to be my dearest friend in football.

The incident in St Etienne is often brought up, but honestly – people need to lighten up! I thought it was hilarious when he scored a late winner, picked up an effigy of me from behind one of the hoardings that he had hidden there before the game, ran to the away crowd with it in his arms, and burned it in front of me!! I mean, that was just good old football-man fun.

The fans are adults, they could make their own minds up about me. Sure, I was a little annoyed when he leaked that story about me being a foot fetishist. Now, I can look back and laugh. The doctored photo that he leaked of me posing in a Paris Saint Germain jersey while holding a sign that said that Marseille fans smelled of cabbage was a JOKE!! I find it sad that people look at these isolated incidents and draw conclusions... that's the press for you, I suppose, but our friendship is as close today as it was when I first met him, shook his hand and moments later wiped his spittle from my chin. Waddle's hilarious 'campaign

of hate' as it was dubbed in the French gutter-press is often cited as the reason for my retirement from the game aged 21. The truth was that I had grown disillusioned with the game. The constant PED use encouraged by the club doctors had put a strain on my libido, and when li'l Ken (that's my penis) is being affected, you know you're on borrowed time.

My personal journal from the time depicts a grim scene. Barricaded into my house because the fans were convinced I wanted out (that scamp Waddle! What a character he was), unable to satisfy my many female companions, and suffering on the pitch, I knew that I must return to my beloved Templeogue. To quote that other tortured Irish genius –

Now that my ladder's gone,
I must lie down where all the
ladders start
In the foul rag and bone shop of
the heart.

Le Monde

Sunday, August 30, 1989

Marseille fans smelled of

Marseille footballeur Ken Early prétend supporters marseillais sentait le chou. Amis et collègues Surprise , envoient des voeux d'anniversaire ou de donner à votre prochain blog poster un look spécial

dire , les mettre sur votre propre site ou blog . S'il vous plaît noter que la liaison directe aux coupures de journaux ne fonctionne pas ; les images sont supprimés du serveur après une courte période de temps .

Pour télécharger votre journal , utilisez le lien au bas de l'image générée

S'il vous plaît ne pa utiliser les noms réels de journaux ou des personn

THE CHOSEN ONES

MOUSTACHES, MULLETS AND MACHISMO: THE GAA'S CULT OF PERSONALITY

Words: Murph

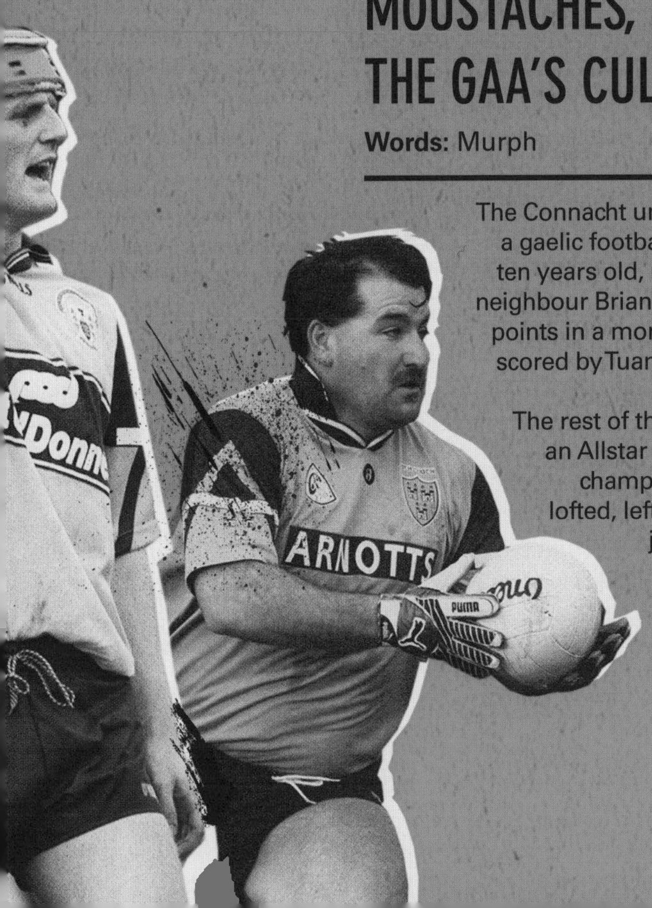

The Connacht under-21 final between Galway and Mayo in 1992 is not a gaelic football story that has grown hackneyed in the telling. I was ten years old, my father was a selector on the Galway team, and my neighbour Brian Forde was Galway captain. Galway won by 1-10 to 12 points in a monsoon, and the only goal of the game was a screamer, scored by Tuam Stars' Jarlath Fallon. He was my first sporting hero.

The rest of the country would soon be acquainted with Ja. He won an Allstar in 1995 after captaining Galway to their first Connacht championship in eight years. He was a scorer of spectacular, lofted, left-footed points, with an almost comically-exaggerated jink and dummy solo that was part-evasion technique, part-epileptic fit.

He would then go on to play a bit of rugby with Connacht, come back to Gaelic football, win an All-Ireland in 1998, tear his cruciate knee ligament, work his way back to fitness and help Galway win a second title in 2001.

That might be considered a reasonable summation of his career, and the career of many sportspeople – ups, downs, awards, glory, failure, injury, recovery, and ultimate fulfilment. But for Galway people of a certain vintage, mention of Ja (both his full first name, and his surname are completely unnecessary) evokes a reaction in the gut and loin area similar to finding in your parents' house the first CD you ever bought and loved.

We love him because he was brilliant. But other footballers on teams he played on were brilliant too, better than Ja was, even at his best. What set him apart? Why was he a cult hero on a team that was almost universally loved?

If you were from Wexford, would you be able to state with absolute confidence that George O'Connor was the best hurler your county had produced during his career? Was Brian Lohan the undisputed best player on the Clare team of the mid-90s? Was John Power a better hurler than DJ Carey? Do the answers to any of those questions actually matter?

The Oxford Dictionary would appear to suggest the one thing that you need to be a cult hero is to be a failure – "a writer, musician, artist, or other public figure who is greatly admired by a relatively small audience or is influential despite limited commercial success."

So that would surely preclude every Kerry footballer ever, right? I asked three separate Kerry people who they would describe as a Kerry footballing cult hero, and all three said - Maurice Fitzgerald. Maurice joined the Kerry football panel two years after the last All-Ireland won by their greatest ever team. He then languished in exile as Kerry won one Munster title in ten years. Was this exquisite torture part of the reason why Maurice came so readily to mind?

MAURICE JOINED THE KERRY FOOTBALL PANEL TWO YEARS AFTER THE LAST ALL-IRELAND WON BY THEIR GREATEST EVER TEAM. HE THEN LANGUISHED IN EXILE AS KERRY WON 1 MUNSTER TITLE IN 10 YEARS.

There appears to be a little wrinkle in the GAA definition of the cult hero. Long periods of anonymous failure might be necessary, but just as vital is the pay-off, the long-awaited platform to show your abilities that comes with winning a few big games in August and September.

There is of course another reason why Maurice's name would come up – and it's not his sublime gifts as a footballer. There is a part of all of us which wishes to see something of ourselves in our heroes. What Kerry person wouldn't say Maurice was the personification of everything good in Kerry football? The hooped socks pulled up to the knee, the languid style, the sheer aesthetic beauty of him gliding over the turf… leaving aside entirely that the history of Kerry football was written every bit as much by players like Paidí Ó Sé and Seamus Moynihan as it was by Mikey Sheehy and Colm Cooper.

If that's what Kerry people want to believe Kerry football is truly about, well of course that's their prerogative. They're the ones doing the cult-ivating here. And it's true that if you look, you'll see plenty of other counties that have anointed men in their own image. The arrogance, the skill, the physicality and the fallibility of Tipperary hurling could be seen writ large in John Leahy's career. Ditto Ciarán Carey in Limerick.

But when I asked Dr Gavin Jennings, Morning Ireland host and regular attendee at Meath O'Byrne Cup fixtures, to pick a cult hero from his time supporting Meath football, he went for David Beggy. Mick Lyons would've seemed to me to have been the obvious pick, but in Gavin's choice there might have been a desire to subvert the traditional view of

Meath football as a rogue's gallery; a pirate-ship of cut-throats, ne'er-do-wells, and Colm Coyle. It's no problem anointing a cult hero in your own image – if you're happy enough with your own image.

Which brings us to Mayo. If Mayo football in the 1980s was a musical genre, it would have been country and western; melancholic, honest, naively charming, its protagonists handsome rather than beautiful. Willie Joe Padden may have been young once (the law of averages would certainly suggest it), but he was always the sort of man your mother would fancy, rather than your sister.

In many ways, Willie Joe is the archetypal GAA cult hero. He is immortalised in song, he played football at 100 miles an hour, he never did something simple when something spectacular would do, and he had a series of physical attributes that set him apart from the ordinary. In Willie Joe's case, those physical attributes (the mullet, the moustache) gave him a rough-hewn allure… and he played an All-Ireland semi-final with a colander on his head, so that's gotta count for something.

But dashing good looks and silky skills are by no means a pre-requisite. Was it Sylvie Linnane's shock of red hair, or his aura of quiet menace, that gave him cult status among Galway hurling fans? Has Francie Bellew a sexual magnetism not immediately apparent to the naked eye, or did his popularity owe more than a passing debt to the whispering death that accompanied his every

move? The inference, with those two and with many others, is that no-one else could love them... and that's why their own fans loved them all the more.

Clare's break-out team in the mid-90s was about as defiant and as charismatic a team as ever won an All-Ireland title. Their captain Anthony Daly was an inspirational leader, straight from the mould of their manager Ger Loughnane. Seanie McMahon and Jamesie O'Connor were artists, as good in their positions as anyone over the last 25 years... but the cult hero in the team was Brian Lohan, the full-back who used his own red helmet as a bellwether for his team's performance.

Throughout that team's history, when the heat would get turned up, Lohan would discard the red helmet at the exact moment when his team's need was greatest; to great, rolling waves of approval from the stand. Jamesie O'Connor remembers the famous red helmet as having had rather dubious safety benefits – "I don't think it was ever fastened too tightly onto him in the first place. But the red helmet was a huge part of it. He just had an incredible aura

about him, in a different way to Daly.

"Maybe it's that wildness; that untamed streak in players that makes them cult heroes. By nature, there are some guys who

are quiet, and there are some guys who just have no respect for authority. I was born in Galway, I grew up watching them in the 1980s and Sylvie had that streak of wildness, or madness, or daring, or boldness in him. And that willingness to play on the edge.

"That was Lohan for us. When Joe Deane got a goal in the 1999 Munster final off Lohan, his helmet fell off and Seanie McGrath kicked it into the net after – I remember thinking 'Jesus, he just disrespected the red helmet!' I asked Lohan about it at training the following Thursday and he said he hadn't noticed.... and yet I definitely got the impression Lohan made a mental note of it for the next time he faced Seanie McGrath."

And sometimes the cult hero has to give the people what they want... even if it's not quite what his teammates wanted at that exact moment. "I remember the 1997 All-Ireland final against Tipperary and as you can imagine it was a pretty intense situation. At one stage in the second half Lohan blew two Tipp lads out of the way, and flicked the ball away. I remember I made a run up the line to ensure an easy 30-40 yard pass but instead Lohan takes a look around him, opens the shoulders

> ## IN ESSENCE THE CULT HERO IS AN INDIVIDUALIST – A PLAYER FOR WHOM THE TEAM ETHIC IS SOMETIMES SACRIFICED AT THE ALTAR OF FREE EXPRESSION.

and blasts it 100 yards down the field. It might have gone harmlessly wide but shur that was the full-forward's fault as far as the crowd were concerned – they nearly lifted the roof off the place."

There is a streak of individualism in the cult hero that one must hope isn't going to be coached into extinction. Brian Lohan's bald-headed runs and long relieving clearances probably wouldn't have much place in the Clare team of

the present day, but then again it wasn't exactly smart play back then either. In essence the cult hero is an individualist – a player for whom the team ethic is sometimes sacrificed at the altar of free expression.

Galway's history of individualists goes back a long way. The legendary newspaperman and broadcaster Jim Carney told me of Tom Sullivan, a Galway player so good that after their

loss in the 1945 All-Ireland semi-final, one national newspaper recorded the final score thus – 'Cork 2-12 Tom Sullivan 2-8'. I'm still not sure I'm any closer to answering the original question – why Ja? – , but if I'd like to think that his high-fielding, his almost Corinthian spirit of fair play, and his flair, sum up all the old guff that Galway people like to associate with our football team, then you'll give me that… right?

SECTION 3

LIVE! LIVE! LIVE!

MCGREGOR

AND IF YOU DON'T KNOW, NOW YOU KNO

PART I

CONOR MCGREGOR HAS RISEN FROM NOWHERE TO BECOME ONE OF THE BIGGEST NAMES IN IRISH SPORT. WHY CAN'T WE GET ENOUGH OF THE FIGHTER FROM CRUMLIN? WE SENT KEN EARLY TO LAS VEGAS TO FIND OUT...

Words: Ken Early

I've just left the emptying Grand Garden Arena and sprinted up to the MGM casino floor. The mental image you have of the big Las Vegas casinos maybe includes green baize tables, roulette wheels, waistcoated croupiers sliding chips around the table with those long rakes, and reveller-gamblers, at least some of whom look glamorous, celebrating their winnings or cursing their bad luck.

Actually, the look and sound of a Vegas casino is totally dominated by slot machines. It's like a maze built of thousands of slot machines, and most of the gamblers are slumped expressionlessly in front of them, moving only the finger that's tapping the bet button. A surprisingly high proportion of these gamblers will have oxygen tubes going into their nostrils and a drink full of floating cigarette butts propped on the console. The casino's atmospheric wallpaper is made up of the blinking flashing lights and repetitive chimes, bleeps and pings of the slots.

But right now I'm not noticing any of that.

There's a famous newspaper correction that goes: "There was an error printed in a story titled 'Pigs Float Down the Dawson' on Page 11 of yesterday's Bully. The story, by reporter Daniel Burdon, said "more than 30,000 pigs were floating down the Dawson river." What Baralaba piggery owner Sid Everingham actually said was "more than 30 sows and pigs", not "more than 30,000 pigs"..."

The scene before me reminds me of that river jammed with 30,000 pigs. The casino floor is a writhing joyous mass of pink Irish flesh, thousands of celebrating fans packed together in the spaces between the slot machines. The fans are swinging their shoes over their heads and singing: "Shoes off for the Boys in Green!"

I'd say this is what it would have been like in Poznan or Sopot if Ireland had actually won a game at the Euros. But it would be more accurate to say this is what it was like in Poznan and Sopot, except this time everyone is indoors and crammed into a much smaller space.

I know this is the Irish tribal sports-drinking-singing ritual that is always the same whether the crowd enacting it is in Poznan or Paradise, NV. But the staff at the MGM Grand fear it and they call the police to chase it away. The cops politely yet firmly set about dispersing the crowd, who are herded, still singing, towards the doors, and out into the hot desert night.

I run the other way because I'm already late for the post-fight press conference.

This event, it turns out, is mainly about Dana White, the manic, hyperverbal President of the Ultimate Fighting Championship. White stands at a podium centre stage and talks and talks. Sitting at long tables either side of him are some of the UFC 189 fighters, tough-looking dudes with bruised faces who look like they'd rather be somewhere else. There's no sign yet of the night's big winner, Conor McGregor.

White is talking about how this might have been the greatest UFC event of all time. I suspect he says that sort of thing about most of the things the UFC has ever done. White doesn't really do understatement.

But this time he might have a point. I tune White out and try to think back over what I've seen.

The first thing that hits you at the fight night is the sound. For most of the five hours or so the fights are going on, gigantic slabs of electro shake the darkened Grand Garden Arena. I've been hearing these tracks all week - Martin Garrix, Pendulum, Dvbbs, Absolut Groovers, The Who. It's trashy Vegas-style EDM-by-numbers, but once you get above a certain volume, quality ceases to matter. At the weigh-ins on Friday afternoon, the excitement overcame a section

of the 15,000-strong Irish crowd; they stripped off their shirts and started bouncing up in the gods like it was the White Horse at 7am on a Sunday morning.

Then there's the visuals. Because most of the people in the arena are too far away from the Octagon to really see what's happening in there, most of them are watching on gigantic HD screens suspended just above. Between fights these are banging out constant promos with images of rippling muscles, tattoos, crunching knockouts, snarling faces, screaming commentators. Everything is geared towards total sensory overload.

I've been to a lot of live sports events and this is the slickest production I've seen. I think back to the Champions League final in Berlin, with its twee opening ceremony and bland corporate trappings. The best

bit of the pre-match had come when the Barcelona end all went "Oooohhoohoohh" to the singalong bit in *Can't Hold Us* by Macklemore & Ryan Lewis. It was cute but hardly the kind of moment to make your head feel like it was about to explode. The presentation of World Cup games is even worse, with the committee-designed FIFA anthem parping out every few minutes.

But the images that linger longest are some of the unproduced, uncut moments from inside the Octagon itself.

I remember a flying knee from the Brazilian bantamweight Thomas Almeida that crunched into the jaw of his opponent Brad Pickett and knocked him out cold. I can't forget the sickening bounce of Pickett's head as he thudded unconscious to the canvas.

It was by far the most stunning piece of violence I've ever seen happen in real life. And I have to admit that part of the reason it made such an impression was that Almeida's move involved a level of skill, power and timing that was comparable to any Neymar bicycle kick.

I remember the moment when Dennis Bermudez opened up the head of Jeremy Stephens with an elbow and I could see the blood pour out as though from a tap. Stephens got up to level Bermudez with another flying knee. Apparently to see two of them in one night is pretty rare, like two players scoring from bicycle kicks in the same match.

I remember the cleaners in the Octagon wiping up the puddle of Stephens' blood while we waited for the welterweight title fight between Robbie Lawler and Rory MacDonald.

That fight turned into a five-round epic that had people in the press box turning to each other in goggle-eyed amazement.

I remember how the blood poured in black rivers down MacDonald's pale face when Lawler burst his nose in the first round.

I remember MacDonald lurching back to his corner and a rope of bloody phlegm dangling from his battered mouth and glinting bright red in the floodlights.

Yeah, all the bits I remember seem to involve blood. I hadn't realised blood had this remarkable mnemonic quality.

People don't agree about what we're watching in the Octagon. Some see a skilled athletic contest between highly-trained athletes with asymetric expertise across a range of sophisticated fighting techniques. Mixed martial arts is a sport that begins with the simple essence of human confrontation and transforms it into a contest of skill, intelligence, courage and strength with

almost infinite tactical variation. The fighters have to put it all on the line, they have to risk real pain and humiliation, they have nowhere to hide. This is sport in its truest form. As Dana White says: "We're humans. Fighting's in our DNA, man."

That sort of talk reminds others of all the Hemingway wank that is spoken about bullfighting which, when you get down to it, is really just cruelty to animals.

THAT SORT OF TALK REMINDS OTHERS OF ALL THE HEMINGWAY WANK THAT IS SPOKEN ABOUT BULLFIGHTING WHICH, WHEN YOU GET DOWN TO IT, IS REALLY JUST CRUELTY TO ANIMALS.

The sceptics see men in tighty whities trying to knee each other in the head while the apes in the stands scream for blood. It's a spectacle that degrades everyone who is party to it. It panders to an ancestral bloodlust that we should be trying to eradicate rather than encourage.

Besides, the haters say, these guys aren't even that good as athletes. If they had serious talent

they'd be in boxing, or football, or some other sport that let them make a lot more money than they're making in there for getting their heads kicked in. It's a disgrace to humanity and it should be banned.

Thankfully for those of us who are at peace with the idea of violence between consenting adults, you can't ban a sport on grounds of taste. What about the argument that it's too dangerous? That one winds up MMA fans, who will tell you to educate yourself. They'll say that boxing is worse, because the count system allows fighters to shake off the immediate effects of a concussion and keep going to sustain further damage. In the UFC, the fight is over the moment you stop "intelligently" defending yourself, so the first concussion you take is also usually the last.

Still, any sport that allows its participants to knee each other in the head has to be dangerous. Dana White is always reminding us nobody has ever died in the UFC. That's true, but it means nothing. Hundreds of people die every year of heart attacks on the golf course. That doesn't mean playing golf is more dangerous than being a UFC fighter. It just means a lot more people are doing it.

Speaking of Dana White, the press conference has gone on for half an hour and I'm wondering if

he's ever going to shut up. Then the door opens and in strolls McGregor, in shiny shades and a shiny dark suit, carrying the shiny 'interim' belt. He sits down, props the belt on the table in front of him, and starts answering questions.

All week I've been watching him strut, preen, bluster and brag. Now, in the immediate aftermath of victory, his demeanour is more thoughtful and subdued than I was expecting. He seems worn out by the intense physical and mental effort of the past few days and barely has the energy to play the showman.

I start to ask a question at the very end, only for White to cut me off - he's objecting that the last question had already been asked - but then he relents and I eventually finish asking the question, something about how McGregor feels at the moment he knocks an opponent out. Someone who knew him had suggested to me earlier in the week that this could be an interesting thing to get him talking about. The exhilarating, and maybe also frightening, emotions that are triggered by the act of reducing another human being to senselessness.

It might well be an interesting question if you had half an hour to tease it out, but right now everyone's too tired to give a shit. McGregor replies that he doesn't take any joy out of knocking people out, but... when you've spent weeks and weeks visualising how you're going to win that fight, it does feel good when you hit the sweet spot.

He's up and heading towards

the door, pausing for a last few photos and he's gone. The journalists sit there typing.

Then something surprising happens. I get a tweet from someone who's apparently been watching the press conference online. Then another, then another. They're from people who recognised my voice asking the question and thought it was funny that Dana White got annoyed with me / Dana White put me in my place / I schooled Dana White, depending on their interpretation. There ends up being at least a dozen of them.

This is weird because it must be eight in the morning in Ireland. Are people seriously sitting there watching the entire fucking post-fight press conference live, an hour of it, all the way to the end? When does that ever happen?

A couple of days later I get a WhatsApp from my sister who's on honeymoon. "Myself and the ball and chain were watchin the press conference with mc Gregor last night...heard your sneaky little question at the end!!"

This is a level of engagement I've never seen before.

***

Back in Dublin, about 30 hours after I saw the pigs in the river, Paul Kimmage was talking

about engaging with the Conor McGregor phenomenon on the Sean O'Rourke show on RTE radio.

"I'm intrigued by it," Kimmage said. "I've been asking about it now for a long time as whether we should engage with this because there is a lot of pantomime to it. It's barbaric. I've watched it and I'm repulsed by it. And I'm thinking 'should the mainstream media engage with

IT'S BARBARIC. I'VE WATCHED IT AND I'M REPULSED BY IT. AND I'M THINKING 'SHOULD THE MAINSTREAM MEDIA ENGAGE WITH THIS?'

this?'. Clearly he has got a lot of support."

Here's some context to help you answer Kimmage's question.

I had written three pieces on the fight for *The Irish Times*. All three featured in the top 10 most-read pieces of that week across *irishtimes.com*, with the fight report being the most-read overall, and they were also the

three most-read pieces on *The Irish Times* sports site across the month of July.

A couple of weeks after the fight, we noticed that the two Second Captains podcasts centred on the McGregor-Mendes fight had become the most popular episodes since we'd started the show in May 2013.

Other media outlets have seen a similar McGregor effect. In July 2014, 3E had recorded a peak audience of 340,000 for McGregor's fight against Diego Brandão. The average audience was more than 257,000, giving them a 21% share (their average share is less than 5%) which included 37% of men aged 15-34, and 43% of all adults aged 15-24.

If you look at TV3's YouTube channel, the third-most-viewed video they've ever published is a fairly bland 10 minute interview with McGregor and coach John Kavanagh on Ireland AM. Only two short clips from the blooper family of virality - "Barack Obama's car gets stuck at government buildings" and "Jack O'Connor walks off Vincent Browne show" - have more views.

JOE.ie developed a commercial relationship with McGregor early in his UFC career, and while the UFC's Reebok sponsorship deal means they can no longer sponsor his ass, they continue to follow McGregor closely, and with good reason. McGregor-Mendes saw their sports site, *sportsJOE.ie*, record what was at that time its biggest day of traffic since its launch in November 2014. The second-biggest was the day before the fight, and the third-biggest was the day after.

cover it more as they realised how hungry the audience was.

Of course, the fact that the audience is interested in something doesn't necessarily mean the mainstream media should cover it. According to *SimilarWeb*, the internet analytics firm, *pornhub.com* attracts more Irish internet users than any Irish

little relevance. The engagement on the mass level has already happened.

So how did Conor McGregor rise from nowhere to become Ireland's most popular sportsman in just a couple of years?

Most people might answer something along the lines of,

$1,182,000

RECORD: 18–2
UFC POINTS: 35
LAST FIVE FIGHTS: 5–0
RECORD VS TOP 10: 1–0
NEXT FIGHT: VS #1 JOSE ALDO

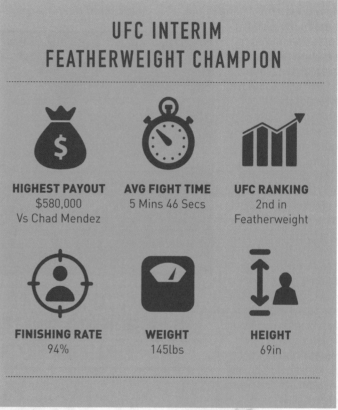

UFC INTERIM FEATHERWEIGHT CHAMPION

HIGHEST PAYOUT	AVG FIGHT TIME	UFC RANKING
$580,000 Vs Chad Mendez	5 Mins 46 Secs	2nd in Featherweight

FINISHING RATE	WEIGHT	HEIGHT
94%	145lbs	69in

Balls.ie also recorded one of their biggest days of traffic on the day of the fight. Their CEO Brian Reynolds says McGregor featured three times in their top 20 stories of the year, and that UFC-related traffic had multiplied 20-fold in the first eight months of 2015 compared to the same period the year before. In part that growth was because *Balls* started to

media website, but that doesn't mean the mainstream media should start publishing more sex videos, even though it would definitely improve audience figures.

It does mean though that mainstream media angst over whether McGregor and his sport is worth engaging with is of

well you know he's something a bit different isn't he - super-confident, looks good, whups ass, not here to take part and all that.

When one interviewer asked McGregor why his fans loved him so much he said: "They love me because I love myself."

Like a few of the lines McGregor

comes out with from time to time, that answer was cleverer than it sounds.

It's not quite true, though. The number one reason why Irish people love McGregor is that he wins. Without winning, none of the other stuff matters.

McGregor now styles himself as the biggest combat sportsman ever to come out of Ireland but that's also not true, at least not yet. Barry McGuigan, Irish boxing's only modern Hall of Famer, was a bigger star in the 1980s than McGregor is now. His world title win against Eusebio Pedroza was watched live by nearly 20 million people in the UK.

McGuigan, like McGregor, fought in an aggressive style that excited people. He was a knockout artist, who had 28 of 32 wins by KO. But his personal style was completely different.

McGregor has a chest tattoo of a gorilla eating a human heart. McGuigan wore a dove of peace on his shorts. He was scrupulously polite, modest and respectful. He didn't hype himself, he didn't insult anyone, he didn't wrap himself in a flag, he didn't boast about how much money he was making. He just turned up and knocked people out.

Of course, McGuigan was a creature of his time and place. Against a backdrop of sectarian killing and hatred, the idea of a

peaceful champion who brought people together had resonance. As Jim Sheridan wrote in his 1985 book about McGuigan: "The people needed a hero who did more than he said."

The time and place where McGregor grew up was ready for a different kind of hero.

In a recent interview to promote The Ultimate Fighter, the UFC's reality show, an American

"I AM WHO I AM, I WAS REARED WHERE I WAS REARED. THAT'S IT. I AM A PRODUCT OF MY ENVIRONMENT, I'M AN IRISHMAN THROUGH AND THROUGH"

reporter asked McGregor if there was something un-Irish about his style, by which they meant the boastfulness, insults, relentless self-aggrandisement etc.

"I am who I am, I was reared where I was reared," McGregor said. "That's it. I am a product of my environment so… I'm an Irishman through and through."

It's interesting to hear McGregor talk to American interviewers about his formative years in

Crumlin, a place where, he says, only two questions matter: "can you fight and can you play football?"

You can see the fascination in their eyes as he describes the mean streets of Dublin 12, where your place in the brutal social hierarchy is determined by the power in your fists. He sometimes makes Crumlin sound like Juarez on the Liffey.

I love listening to these stories because I lived in Crumlin for seven years and it's really a very normal, quiet, boring suburb. The youth of Crumlin is distinguished less for its martial fervour than for its love of smoking weed and playing FIFA.

A friend from Crumlin who played football with McGregor years ago describes a quiet, unassuming kid with white-blond hair in a bowl haircut - just a normal kid, one of the lads. But a tale of conventional suburban normality doesn't quite fit the creation myth of the Notorious One. The fight game expects backstory. The young Mike Tyson, driven to violence for the first time when a guy ripped the head off one of his pigeons, that sort of stuff.

The truth is that Crumlin is plagued by something, but it's not the ever-present threat of violence. The problem is the dullness, the featurelessness.

CONTINUED ON PAGE 90 >>>

SECOND CAPTAINS

JOHN MULLANE

DANIEL-SAN

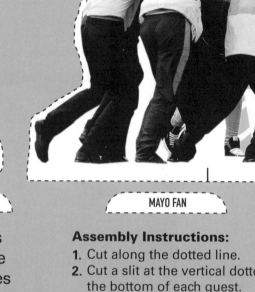

MAYO FAN

Wow! It's a Second Captains Sports Dinner Party at your fingertips! Invite some of the most entertaining names from the world of sport to join you for a top-class sporting soirée! In your own house! Terrible cook? Don't worry, I can't see this lot sending their food back to the chef! No fights, no complaints, no awkward silences, just a night of sports chat* with some sport #celebs!
Tuck in!

*you must do most of the chat.

Assembly Instructions:
1. Cut along the dotted line.
2. Cut a slit at the vertical dotted line on the bottom of each guest.
3. Cut the name along the dotted line.
4. Insert the name card into the vertical slit.
5. Pick what guests you want to invite to your sports dinner party.
6. Make excuses to guests you don't want to invite.
7. Stand up guests around your dinner table.
8. Enjoy your dinner.

SPORTS DINNER PARTY

KEN EARLY

PEIG SAYERS

JOHN REGIS

THE GUESTS: What They Bring

John Mullane – Has his own branded Second Captains tea towels to mop up any spills. Will bring more passion to the dinner table than anyone else and loves spuds

Daniel-San LaRusso – Has top fancy dress party credentials but may shite on about Cobra Kai a bit

Mayo Fan V Kerry 2014 – Just make sure you cook the dinner right

Ken Early – Perhaps use the flame-haired, flame-thrower of truth as dinner party debate moderator? Make sure the wine cellar is stocked

Peig Sayers – Road bowling legend but not much craic let's be honest

John Regis – Find out what really made Roger Black tick from the man with the biggest chest in sports history

Let them ask
Cake

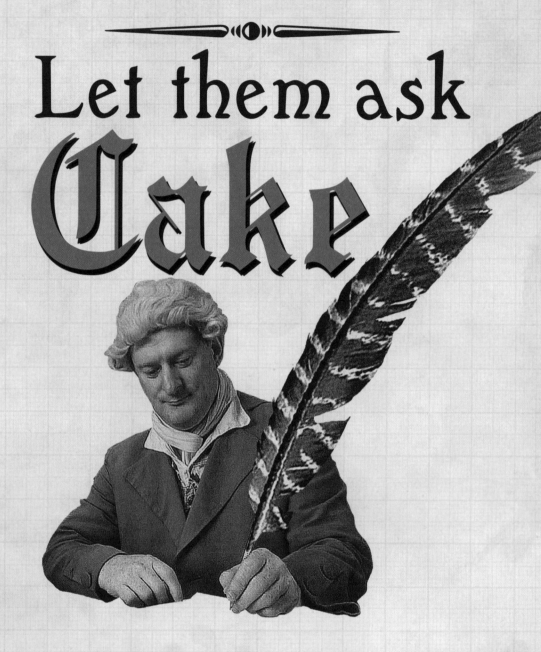

Relationship and sporting advice from
Roscommon's greatest-ever goalkeeper,
Shane 'Cake' Curran.

Q Howya Cake,
I've got a question for you, goalie to goalie… are the days of us getting away with wearing rugby boots over? I'm in Munster but I'd rather not give my name…

A Cake says – don't be daft. As long as there's a hole in me arse there'll be a place for rugby boots in the GAA. They feel good, they look good, and most importantly they mark you out as a lunatic.

Q Cake,
I brought my new boyfriend to a hotel down the country recently for his birthday. Everything was going well until after breakfast on our first morning. He returned to the buffet area in the breakfast room and proceeded to put as many items of food as he possibly could into his bag "for later in the day." I was disgusted as this to me is stealing. What do I do?
- Cathy from Naas.

A Well Cathy, it's simple. You can't be piling rashers or black puddin' or any cooked food into a bag for later. You can't be filling your bag up with food if you're in a small little B&B. BUT if you were in a big hotel and your new man was taking an apple or two, a few old rolls, a slice of ham and a yoghurt for himself and yourself? Well then I'd say he's a keeper. That's not stealing, that's just abiding by an unwritten hotel law.

Q Hey Cake,
Do you ever look up at the sky at night, maybe after you've had a few pints, and see all the stars shining in the darkness,

the light of long-dead stars reaching us across the millennia, the cosmos in all its magnificence and glory, and think about how small and puny and insignificant we all are?
- Liam in Wexford.

A No.

Q Cake. When supporting the Rossies I'm never sure whether to tuck the shirt into my cut-off denims or just tie it into a knot on my waist, thereby revealing my belly tattoo of Francie Grehan's face.
- Diarmuid, 24 hours from Tulsk

A Tuck it in Diarmuid. Through a chink too wide, comes in no wonder, as Francie himself says.

Q Hey Cake. Is there anything else Taylor Swift could do to make things up with Nicki Minaj or is there too much water under the bridge at this stage? It seems so avoidable, I hate to see them squabble like they have done in 2015. - Rupert, Longford.

A I find it really hard to solve my celebrity feuds when everyone else is putting their oar in. Let them at it. That said, I am a fully signed up member of Barbz, so you know where my allegiances lie.

Q Cake,
What is your favourite type of cake?

A Romantica ice-cream cake.

Q Shane I need your help. I'm a small balding man of 19 years of age. I reckon I've three more years left until the hair has gone fully Hulk Hogan or Michael D. Higgins. Do I shave it off now and just give up and hopefully people will think it's a style decision? Or do I take my chances and hope this balding phase will slow?
- PJ, Longford.

A PJ, first of all there's not a thing wrong with being bald, it never held back Christy Ring or Fabien Barthez. But you do have to take decisive action. Your balding is not going to slow down so get that razor out and take control.

Q Cake,
What would be your death-row meal? I'm talking five courses here with no expense spared followed by any pint of your choice before death by the lethal injection of a dose of intravenously administered drugs (for murder)?

A Seeing as I'm on death row about to be killed, I presume I'm in America. Therefore, I'd choose produce and cuisine of a local nature starting with a bowl of buffalo wings. Next up a juicy hamburger. To remind me of home I'd have steak and a few spuds before some Romantica ice-cream and an Irish coffee to finish. Nice pint of Guinness and I'd be off!

Have a family problem, troubled romance, or a fashion-related question? Send your scroll to editor@secondcaptains.com

RIO OLYMPICS 2016
THE KIM

COLLINS EFFECT

Words: Amy O'Connor

A HEAD OF NEXT YEAR'S OLYMPICS IN RIO DE JANEIRO, AMY O'CONNOR TELLS US HOW THE GAMES EMOTIONALLY CONNECT US TO AN UNLIKELY CAST OF CHARACTERS, AND THE STRANGEST AND MOST OBSCURE OF SPORTS, FOR TWO WEEKS EVERY FOUR YEARS.

Next year, the 31st edition of the Summer Olympic Games will take place in Rio, Brazil. Like many sports nerds, I am positively giddy at the prospect of spending a fortnight indoors watching sports. Cheering on your fellow countrymen as you lie on the couch in your 'around-the-house' pants, getting emotionally invested in table tennis and rhythmic gymnastics, bristling every time you hear the term 'Team GB' - it's all part and parcel of the Olympics.

But perhaps my favourite feature of the Olympics is being reunited with the cast of characters you met four years before — the athletes, the studio pundits, the commentators. Like Kim Collins.

Kim Collins is a decorated sprinter from Saint Kitts and Nevis, a tiny two-island nation tucked away in the West Indies. Since he first competed in the 1996 Olympic Games, he has won a World Championship in the men's 100m and competed in 100 metres and 200 metres finals in the Olympics.

Despite never quite managing to sneak his way on to the Olympic podium, he has almost always been on the starting line. To put it in Hollywood terms, if he were an actor, he would be Steve Buscemi or Paul Giamatti — someone you're always pleased to see, but is never really the main attraction.

I can't pinpoint exactly when my obsession with Kim Collins began, although I do remember my mother once remarking, "Kim Collins? He sounds like he could be from Cork." Since then, I have rooted for him at every available opportunity. After all, there is something irresistible and improbable about a man from the smallest country in the Western Hemisphere having a real shot at being crowned the fastest man in the world.

Yes, for two weeks every four years, I form an inexplicable attachment to Kim Collins and others like him. But once the Olympics conclude and normal service resumes, they vanish from my thoughts and I don't think about them again until the next Olympiad rolls around. I call this phenomenon "The Kim Collins Effect".

Think about it. When was the last time you took a moment to ponder the legacy of Moroccan middle distance runner Hicham El Guerrouj? Have you paused recently to reminisce about Gabby Douglas making history and becoming the first African-American gymnast to win gold? When did you last stop in your steps, Angelus style, to really think about Philips Idowu's brightly coloured hair?

I'm going to go out on a limb and guess that your answer to all of these questions is either, "Who?" or "Oh yeah, that guy!"

YES, FOR TWO WEEKS EVERY FOUR YEARS, I FORM AN INEXPLICABLE ATTACHMENT TO KIM COLLINS AND OTHERS LIKE HIM.

And it's not just athletes that fall prey to the Kim Collins Effect. Commentators and studio pundits — the voices who help shape and form your sporting memories, and live on in perpetuity on *Reeling in the Years* reruns— are victims of this phenomenon, too. For a few weeks every four years, people like swimming expert Gary O'Toole and exhuberant basketall commentator Timmy 'Downtown' McCarthy are treated like sporting sages. Myles Dungan gets to show off his vast sporting knowledge and remind everyone, "Hey, not only am I a bloody good historian, but I am also a highly competent sailing commentator." And one-time Olympic hopefuls begin their transition into broadcasting and pray that they can become the next Steve Cram.

But while these people are as much a part of the sporting experience as the athletes — at least from the spectator's point of view — they're as good as forgotten once the Games are over, relegated to the sidelines of sports punditry.

You see, the Olympics is unique in the way it facilitates a deep yet fleeting bond between the viewer and its cast of characters. Over the space of a month, you become intimately aware of the obstacles each athlete has overcome to be there. You're given the lowdown on injuries, personal setbacks, controversies. You're spoonfed soundbites like, "A victory here would mean so much to her!" And before you know it, you're squeezing a stress ball and roaring like a fisherwoman at the Cuban triple jumper on your TV screen.

Likewise, people like the late Bill O'Herlihy or the BBC's Gabby Logan shepherd you through the Olympic coverage and become such a fixture in your everyday life that you almost come to regard them as friends, chuckling to yourself at the studio banter that you're watching from your couch. "That Michael Johnson," you think to yourself. "What a hoot."

For a brief period, these people hog headlines, generate watercooler moments and burrow their way into your heart. You find yourself celebrating victories, commiserating with fourth place finishers and feeling prehistoric when a 17-year-old child wins a gold medal. You may even delude yourself into thinking that you're going to start following athletics, swimming, or badminton properly now. But then it ends and they become all but a distant memory. It's almost like being at an intense weekend session where you vow to keep in touch with all the beautiful strangers you've just met, only to promptly forget about them all the next morning.

And next August, we'll do it all again. For a fortnight, we'll fall in love with obscure Olympians for arbitrary reasons. We'll marvel at how good-looking Brazilians are. We'll tweet glorious non-sequiturs like, "YES USAIN" and "!!!!!" We'll harbour delusions that maybe, just maybe, Ireland can win a gold in track and field. And we'll cheer on the underdogs like Kim Collins, who, as of writing, fully intends on competing in the Games.

It'll be magic. And I don't know about you, but I can't bloody wait.

@amyohconnor

OTHER EXAMPLES OF THE KIM COLLINS EFFECT

Frankie Fredericks

With a name that suggests he was spinning house records in Chicago in the early 1980s, Frankie Fredericks is widely regarded as one of the nicest guys in athletics. He may not have ever set a world record or won an Olympic gold, but the Namibian sprinter won four silver medals throughout his career. And, more importantly, he won his way *into our hearts.*

Laszlo Cseh

The baby-faced Hungarian has been a fixture on the swimming circuit for years and his intense gaze will no doubt be familiar to anyone who stayed up until the wee hours during the 2008 Olympics to see Michael Phelps complete his medal haul. Unfortunately for Cseh, he finished second to Phelps in three separate events. Sport: it's a cruel mistress.

Beth Tweddle

Gymnastics has a notoriously high turnover -- every four years, you're met with a crop of impossibly youthful faces. One of the few faces you could always depend on to pop up in recent years, though, was good ol' Beth Tweddle, a British gymnast who was never put under any pressure by the British media, nope, no way.

Eric Moussambani

In 2000, Eric Moussambani of Equitorial New Guinea became a minor celebrity when he swam 100m in the spectacularly slow time of 1:52. (No, this is not the plot of a *Cool Runnings*-esque film. This is real life.) The press christened him Eric The Eel, he became the breakout star of the Sydney Olympics and the rest is history.

TEARS OF A CLOWN

There is no nobler aim in life than the well-delivered costume-based visual gag. It has been our privilege over the last two years on **Second Captains Live** on RTE 2 to gently skewer the Irish political and chattering classes via biting satire... and competitively-priced, highly-flammable Hallowe'en costumes.

The blank (-faced) canvas upon which we have painted their sartorial pictures is well-known clothes-hanger Ciaran 'Murph' Murphy.

Here now, we present the behind-the-scenes story of how these costumes came to be made...

1.

1. Murph as the Wavin pipe endorsing Denis Hickie

Sandy Ductstein, Wavin pipe expert and marketing executive - When I saw his elaborate entrance into studio, I just thought 'wow'. All any of us guys at Wavin could talk about after this episode was "why didn't WE think of this?" A sportsman harnessing all the awesome power of the renowned market-leader in the pipe and land drainage game to create a kind of robo-sportsman? It made perfect sense. We have already begun negotiations for a new version of the ad featuring Mike Ross and our new jumbo industrial pipe range. Thanks Second Captains!

Ciaran Murphy, television star – I took a seemingly perfect TV advertisement to a new level, I easily defeated Oisin McConville AND I got to sit down with some Irish sporting royalty whilst dressed as a Wavin pipe. THIS was my proudest ever moment. Even if it was tricky explaining myself to David Forde afterwards.

2. Murph as FAI former mascot, Irish wolfhound Macúl

Ciaran Murphy, television star - "As you can see from the pictures, it can sometimes be chaotic backstage as I attempt to change during an ad break. But sometimes I get a chance to take a moment and just be thankful for how far I've come in my career. Sure we couldn't get a wolfhound suit, but I won't hear a bad word about the cheap wolf alternative. It allowed me to take the ball down expertly on my wolf-chest, send the keeper the wrong way whilst maintaining balance with my wolf-tail, and score the greatest goal on Irish TV of 2015."

3. Murph as the voyeuristic GAA Cow

Karen Reen, SC Live production manager – "Two things that really concerned us with this one were 1) the size of his cow-horns, and 2) the quality of hoof. He was going to kick a point so the hooves had to be really top-class. We eventually went with a top half from a well-known Swiss fashion-house, and made the bottom half ourselves, using a Kevlar under-carriage and a pair of used Gola runners. Murph nearly backed out of this one but thankfully Mark Horgan convinced him of how important this unfinished journalistic work was."

4. Murph as celebrating hat-trick hero Don Givens v USSR in 1974

Ken Early, co-host – "This was a really tough one for us because of the respect that we all have for Don. So we were anxious that this costume capture the magnificence of his celebrations (and hair) on that famous night in '74. What people don't know is that they were not actually Murph's real hands! Fake hands were in fact sown onto an old Ireland jersey, Murph was then clad in said jersey, he hammered Richie Sadlier in the quiz and the rest as they say is TELEVISION HISTORY."

5. Murph as jockey/mooner Blake Shinn

Mark Horgan, series producer – "A little known fact about Murph is that he is extremely anxious about the hairiness of his arse. All the talk in the run-up to this episode centred on whether he would waive the no-nudity clause in his contract. He went back and forth on it for days but when he finally decided to completely shave and then bare his ACTUAL arse, it was one of the real journalistic triumphs of series 4."

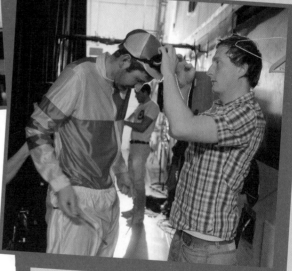

KEN EARLY'S DOODLEPAD:
Murph Portraits

1. Reflections In a Dullard's Eye

2. Indignities of Middle Age

3. The Vacuity of a Face

AWKWARD PHOTOSHOOTS

STARRING KEN EARLY

WE'LL LET YOU IN ON A SECRET. KEN EARLY HATES PHOTOSHOOTS.

Forget cutting comebacks from Steve Staunton or on-air dorky duels with football correspondents from around the globe, Ken's at his most uncomfortable when he's the centre of attention, posing awkwardly in a variety of stupid situations and positions.

With this in mind, here's the **Second Captains Top 5 photographs of Ken posing awkwardly in stupid situations and positions.**

2.

SMILE OF PAIN
Ken poses with a photo of Liam Brady (as directed) whilst secretly wanting to kill his colleagues.

1.

DEAD BEHIND THE EYES
Ken puts a ball on his head, as directed.

3.

FUCK YOU FOR MAKING ME DO THIS
Ken asks himself "where did it all go wrong?" whilst dressing up as 90s boyband member, as directed.

4.

CAN'T GO ANY LOWER
Ken lying on the floor, as directed.

5.

BLOW CRY
Ken gets his hair prepared as he poses as an East
German 1970s footballer, as directed.

SECTION 4

TERRY
MONAGHAN
TRIES YOGA!?

<<< CONTINUED FROM PAGE 73

PART II
MCGREGOR
AND IF YOU DON'T KNOW, NOW YOU KNOW

Like so many other boring Dublin suburbs, there isn't a lot for a kid to do but get baked, drink cans, play Xbox and watch documentaries on DMAX.

So growing up in Crumlin probably didn't give McGregor his thirst for combat, but there were probably a few times when he was walking around thinking to himself: is this all there is?

***

If he was thinking that, he wasn't alone.

In March and April of 2013 my colleagues and I enjoyed a period of gardening leave that left us with plenty of time to wander aimlessly around the streets of Dublin. At some point it struck us that town was crawling with what we would later call on the podcast 'The Muscly Young Men of Ireland'.

It was an unusually warm spring and there suddenly seemed to be a lot of guys out walking around in muscle vests to show off suspiciously inflated, gym-honed physiques.

Being young in Dublin used to be about drinking cans and smoking hash with bits of plastic in it, but now it seemed the thing to do was to pump iron and get ripped. If these guys were taking drugs it was creatine or maybe something a bit stronger than that. Some of them were probably serious fitness nuts, into triathlon or MMA or whatever, hooked on natural endorphins and finding an almost religious meaning and purpose in the discipline of training - a bit like the young McGregor.

Then again, a lot of the muscley young men didn't look like proper athletes. They looked like guys who were trying to get ripped for the specific purpose of looking ripped.

There was another cultural landmark later that year when then-Liverpool manager Brendan Rodgers returned from the summer break with a dazzling new smile, a rich mahogany tan, and pecs rippling where moobs had once threatened to swell.

Cosmetic enhancement seemed a curious way to channel the spirit of Bill Shankly. Whatever qualities had enabled Shankly to build Liverpool into a bastion of invincibility, they didn't have much to do with pearly whites and killer abs. A hostile internet mocked Rodgers' vanity.

But you had to think about it from Rodgers' point of view. His life changed when he became the manager of Liverpool. Among the more disconcerting changes was that he suddenly realised he was all over TV and the internet every single day. Imagine every time you looked at a screen you saw your own pallid face, dimpled hands, and yellow crooked-toothed grin looking back at you. You're rich enough to change it with a phone call - what would you do?

Rodgers, like Jurgen Klopp, the hair-transplanted German who would replace him at Anfield, decided that the taboo on real men having work done need no longer apply.

The muscly young men of Ireland and Brendan Rodgers alike are responding to the same cultural forces. Not many of them were on TV every day like Rodgers, but they do appear every day on a lot of screens, screens belonging to themselves and everybody they know.

There was a time not long ago when a lot of us might have seen ourselves once in the morning and once again in the evening when we were brushing our teeth, if we fancied ourselves enough to bother with that stuff. You might have an occasional Thomas Kinsella moment: 'wow, I really look like shit today'. But it was easy to put that out of your mind because the world seldom forced you to look at yourself.

Then, in just a couple of years, we all got phones that allowed us to take unlimited numbers of free, high quality photos and videos and share them with everyone we know on the internet.

For whatever reason, people seem to have got more concerned about the way they look. If everyone didn't have an 8-megapixel camera in their pocket, do you really think Centra would be selling protein powders?

It's only ten years since the social networks began the project of connecting everyone in the world. The revolution was always going to have some unintended consequences. It turns out that in connecting with each other we became separated from ourselves.

Gabriel Garcia Marquez wrote that everyone had three selves: public, private, and secret. Social media has generated a fourth layer: the digital self - an external entity that exists in the abstract space of the internet, a creature that looks like us, made out of images and comments, a thing we can shape but not fully control. The digital self is the version of the self that most other people see, and it's increasingly the one that people care about most.

The structure of social media equates status with attention. Likes, retweets, friends and followers are all measures of attention, and though they're not explicitly presented as proxies for social success, that's how we tend to look at them.

This is transforming the way we relate to each other. If the highest goal in life is attention, then any private thought or moment that remains unshared is a tree that falls in a lonely forest. Privacy is a waste.

Everything becomes about display. In Ireland especially, self-promotion was once considered to be in poor taste. Now, for large swathes of the population, it's not embarrassing, just logical. Modesty and humility used to be marks of good character. Now they're just short-cuts to oblivion.

If a bunch of digital marketing people sat down to design a sportsman to incarnate the spirit of the time, an incredibly ripped, mouthy martial arts guy who unselfconsciously describes

himself as a "new breed of bad motherfucker" - well, that guy would tick every box.

Not that there was anything manufactured about McGregor when he first started to get famous.

***

The first time I heard of him was just before his first UFC fight in March 2013. That was during the unemployment/gardening leave phase, when we spent a

lot of time in the house of our producer, Mark Horgan, trying to figure out our next move.

One of those days Mark was watching some videos on YouTube and at some point I became aware of what is now a familiar voice, shouting out over the tinny laptop speakers.

"We're broke-ass motherfuckers over here, you know what I mean, all us Irish guys training over here 24-7, haven't got a pot to piss in! So I wanna bring shows over here for all us guys, so we can ALL get paid!"

It was an episode of *The MMA Hour* with Ariel Helwani and there on the screen, via Skype from Dublin, was Conor McGregor, who was about to make his UFC debut in Stockholm against Marcus Brimage. Both host and guest were clearly having fun doing this interview.

Every so often McGregor was popping some little stuff into his mouth and Helwani asks to know what he's eating.

"Blueberries!" McGregor shouts. "Fucking DE-LIC-IOUS! I'm a lean motherfucker as well! Lean as they come!" He throws his head back and laughs in a manic high-pitched cackle.

McGregor knocked Brimage out in the first round and a few days later he was back on with Helwani.

He was still on a massive high from the victory, loving life, crackling with energy and enthusiasm. He never stopped smiling. He told Helwani that until the week before he'd been living on social welfare. For the first time in his life he's had to open a bank account.

McGregor had done a bit of what has become his trademark trashtalk and posturing during the build-up and Helwani wanted to know more about it. "I'm just playing up," McGregor replied, "it's like the WWE you know… it's all a game."

Helwani seemed surprised by McGregor's casually knowing tone. "You know, people like to buy that stuff, they like to eat that up. Is it good to admit that?"

McGregor sounded like he hadn't been asked that question before. "Yeah… I dunno, I don't really give a shit. You know what I mean? It's not gonna make a difference. All them motherfuckers are still gonna pay for their ticket, trust me on that." Another high pitched cackle.

The goofy exuberance peaked when Helwani asked him about his special chicken pizza recipe. "That is the nicest paleo dish you're ever gonna get!" he shouts. "What you do is, you get three chicken fillets, and an egg, raw, yeah, you put it into a food processor, wazz it up with a little garlic and a little chilli powder, and make it into like a snot, it literally goes like snot, yeah? And take it out then and put it into a tray, put it out like a base of a pizza, stick it into the oven 15 minutes, take it out, wazz up some tomatoes in the food processor, chilli paste and tomato paste and fresh basil.

Butter or… put the sauce on top of the pizza, on top of the chicken base - and then start packing it with more shit! I put like, lamb mince, chicken sausages, avocado, onions, peppers, chickpeas! Stuck it back in the oven for 15-20 minutes more, and it was the Fuckin'. Nicest. Thing I've ever had in me life! You know Shredder Joe's, that could be Shredder Joe's signature dish! Lean and clean yeah!" He cackles with delight.

Two and a half years on we've reached the point where it seems like it would be impossible to watch all the Conor McGregor content on YouTube in a single human lifespan.

The UFC encourages this proliferation and manufactures a lot of it in-house. The commercial model is to charge big money for the monthly PPV events, broadcast the lesser events as widely as possible on free-to-air TV, and feed the interest by churning out massive quantities

of promotional material which everyone can watch for free online.

To promote UFC 189, the UFC conceived an eight-city international tour in which McGregor and Aldo would travel to key markets facing off and talking smack. On March 31st, the roadshow rolled into Dublin for a press conference at the National Convention Centre.

White came on stage wearing an Ireland football shirt and instantly had the crowd eating out of his hand. "Fifteen years I've been doing this and I've never seen any shit like Dublin!" he yelled. Not subtle, but the crowd lapped it up.

McGregor gave them more of what they wanted. Aldo droned on through an interpreter, while McGregor gleefully acted the maggot. When Aldo's interpreter said something about how Aldo was the King of Dublin, McGregor threw his feet up on the table and shouted "You're lookin' at the King of Dublin!"

Dublin didn't use to be the kind of town that loved people who claimed to be its King. It is now. The crowd went nuts. Emboldened by all the aggressive energy McGregor jumped up and snatched Aldo's belt, and the crowd loved that even more.

The UFC like to round off these events by inviting the fans to ask the fighters some questions. Jose Aldo - an undefeated champion, rated the best pound-for-pound fighter in the UFC - was forced

CONTINUED OVER >>>

TOP TEAMS COOL ON TERRY AS FANS HEAT UP
TERRY DOES AN ALL EXCLUSIVE INTERVIEW WITH GARTH CROOKS ON FOOTBALL FOCUS
FOR NOW GARTH, I'M A WEST HAM PLAYER. OF COURSE IT WOULD BE A DREAM TO PLAY WITH A MARGINALLY BIGGER CLUB GETTING PAID WAY BIGGER MONEY, BUT I DON'T KNOW WHERE THESE STORIES ARE COMING FROM...
THEN
TERRY THE TRAITOR
A WEST HAM FAN LIGHTS HIMSELF ON FIRE IN FRONT OF TERRY'S HOUSE
MEANWHILE
TERRY SIGNS A NEW CONTRACT WITH WEST HAM
GO TO PAGE 99

to sit and stare while Irish lads queued up to insult him.
"Aldo - eighteen fights in ten years, what's that, one and a half fucking fights a year - you're SHIT mate. McGregooor!"

"Fanny! You're his bitch, Aldo! Aldo, you bitch!"

"You've got 3,000 Irish lads here, red-blooded, tell us, we wanna know, what does Jose's pussy smell like?"

And so on.

If you mention this press conference to anyone involved with the MMA scene in Ireland they cringe. It was excruciating for them because it created the impression that MMA was a sport supported by arseholes and idiots.

McGregor laughed his way through the Q&A but you wondered if part of him was a little freaked out by what was happening. The bandwagon he had set in motion was gathering its own momentum.

A lot of these fans were crude copies of McGregor himself, imitating his look - beards, shades, tattoos, undercuts tied up in a little bun - and also what they understood to be his attitude - loud, disrespectful, confrontational, obnoxious. That might have been more of an ego boost for McGregor if they hadn't also been unfunny, untalented, ignorant and moronic. How does it feel to see masses of people trying to be you, but doing it really badly?

Watching him ham it up on stage you started to wonder, was McGregor still in charge of his own circus? Or had he become a dancing monkey pandering to the impulses of the crowd? Was he controlling them, or were they controlling him?

***

In the summer of 2013, McGregor did an interview with Fox where they asked him how he was spending his newly-acquired riches.

"You ever hear the saying, 'It's hard to get up and run when you're wearing silk underwear?' Like you get rich, and you lose your hunger? Well I've got a foolproof plan. When you get your money, spend every penny of it! Blow it all! Until you're actually broke come the next fight! So you're just as hungry as you were. So, I'm in the process of blowing every penny of that."

McGregor immediately settled into a kind of Notorious BIG in *Juicy* lifestyle. Suits, jewellery, cars, expensive whiskey, all the usual stuff you never knew you wanted until you suddenly had a load of money you didn't know what to do with.

As you would expect, a couple of years of this has had an effect on his personality. He's no longer a guy who you can imagine getting excited about liquidised chicken that looks like snot. Now he usually appears in shades and something shiny and tailored, wearing a jewel-encrusted watch, sitting with his head tilted back, jaw set, haughty as a Mount Rushmore head, boasting about how much richer he is than all the other bums.

Mostly he talks about money and his focus has changed to accumulating rather than dissipating his fortune. "I am in it for the gold and the cash, make no mistake… my favourite pastimes are shopping and counting."

He seldom breaks character any more, and you have a sinking feeling that he might be starting to believe this amped-up persona is actually the real him. But the new, 'shopping and counting' McGregor continues to attract more and more attention: if it ain't broke, why fix it?

All the money talk, whether it's just a provocative promotional device or a genuine obsession, does leave you wondering: how much money can you actually make in the UFC?

The basic contract for a fighter starting out in the company is eight and eight - $8,000 to fight, and an $8,000 bonus to win. If you fight particularly well you might earn a bonus for the best knockout or the best performance of the night. And if you can develop momentum and a following, you can expect your basic contract to improve.

McGregor's total disclosed earnings from his six UFC fights amount to $1,182,000 - which is not bad for a guy who started 2013 on the dole. And there are plenty of other, undisclosed, revenue streams. He was credited as executive producer on *The Notorious* documentary series that was screened in Ireland on RTE and sold in several overseas territories. And then there was sponsorship, ads, commercial and corporate appearances, undisclosed bonuses, and so on.

Still, this is not serious money - what you might call Wayne Bridge money. McGregor's direct earnings from two and a half years and six fights in UFC had earned him roughly what Wayne Bridge earned in two months training with Man City's reserves, or what Floyd Mayweather earned to share the ring with Manny Pacquiao for fifteen seconds.

The serious money in UFC comes when you start to headline pay-per-view events. Then you can expect a cut of the PPV take, though these figures are not disclosed. Dana White claimed that Jose Aldo could have made up to four million dollars if he'd turned up to fight McGregor, though we only have his word for it.

McGregor has now reached that elite stage. With a few more wins at this level he will make many millions of dollars.

But there's nothing like hanging around with really rich people to make you feel poor.

***

Dana White once dreamed of being a boxer, but realised in early adulthood that his real gift was for promoting and the art of bullshit in general. In 2001, White

clubbed together with his rich Vegas buddies Lorenzo and Frank Fertitta and bought the UFC.

The Fertitta brothers are billionaire casino owners who have the typical billionaire's attitude to publicity. They mostly stayed in the background while White became the public face and voice of the organisation.

White has explained that when they were deciding how to run the UFC, "boxing was our model of what NOT to do."

Where boxing is a shambolic tangle of associations and belts, the UFC provides a clear and unified competitive structure. While boxing promoters depend on the brands of individual boxers to sell the fights, the UFC has developed a brand that can sell out arenas from Stockholm to Sydney.

That's all smart. Still, you suspect that the biggest issue White & the Fertittas had with boxing is that in boxing, most of the money goes to the boxers.

Most people think it's reasonable that a large proportion of the money that flows into professional sport should end up in the pockets of professional sportsmen. That's how it works in most sports. Players in the NFL, NBA, NHL and MLB all take home around 50% of the total revenues of the league. In the Premier League, the players get 58% of overall revenues, which is how Steven Fletcher gets to have a Lamborghini Aventador.

When Floyd Mayweather fought Manny Pacquiao, the two fighters took home around 66% of the total revenue generated by the fight.

The UFC's business model must be the envy of wealthy owners in every sport, because less than 10% of the UFC's near-$500 million annual revenue goes to the actual fighters themselves. That means the only people in the sport making what you could call Jorge Mendes money are Dana White and the Fertitta brothers.

Their model is all about taking as much as possible of the value

MCGREGOR CAREER EARNINGS BREAKDOWN

V CHAD MENDES	V DENNIS SIVER	V DUSTIN POIRIER	V DIEGO BRANDÃO	V MAX HOLLOWAY	V MARCUS BRIMAGE
JULY 2015, LAS VEGAS	JANUARY 2015, BOSTON	SEPTEMBER 2014, LAS VEGAS	JULY 2014, DUBLIN	AUGUST 2013, BOSTON	APRIL 2013, FUEL TV

UFC 189 TOTAL EARNINGS	UFC FIGHT NIGHT TOTAL EARNINGS	UFC 178 TOTAL EARNINGS	UFC FIGHT NIGHT TOTAL EARNINGS	UFC FIGHT NIGHT TOTAL EARNINGS	UFC ON FUEL TV TOTAL EARNINGS
$580,000	**$220,000**	**$200,000**	**$82,000**	**$24,000**	**$76,000**

BREAKDOWN	BREAKDOWN	BREAKDOWN	BREAKDOWN	BREAKDOWN	BREAKDOWN
SALARY: $500,000	SALARY: $85,000	SALARY: $75,000	SALARY: $16,000	SALARY: $12,000	SALARY: $8,000
PON: $50,000	WIN BONUS: $85,000	WIN BONUS: $75,000	WIN BONUS: $16,000	WIN BONUS: $12,000	WIN BONUS: $8,000
SPONSORSHIP: $30,000	PON BONUS: $50,000	PON BONUS: $50,000	PON BONUS: $50,000		KOOTN BONUS: $60,000

created by the fighters, and packing it into the brand they control. In every other sport, the best players are the biggest stars. The biggest star in the UFC is Dana White.

McGregor earned well out of UFC 189, but at the other end of the scale the Irish fighter Neil Seery took home $10,000, out of which he had to pay his cornermen and various other expenses.

At the UFC 189 closing press conference, an excited White was talking about the incredible brutality of the fight between Robbie Lawler and Rory MacDonald. "Robbie Lawler's lip - if you could have been in the Octagon and saw this lip - he would talk, this part of the lip would move and this wouldn't… And whatsisname's nose was broken…"

Earlier that night I had watched whatsisname stagger past my desk, physically and spiritually

shattered, with blood still oozing from his pulped face. For this he had earned $59,000, which was later bumped up to $109,000 with a Fight of the Night bonus because nobody had ever seen anyone take such a beating. You can be sure whatsisname's suffering had helped make more than $109,000 for White that week.

MMA is a sport that demands a lot from its athletes: hard training, strict diet, traumatic weight cuts, all leading up to the possibility of a savage beating. After all that sacrifice it can seem surprising that the fighters are apparently prepared to accept financial exploitation too.

You have to remember that the players in America's other sports didn't achieve a 50% revenue split with their leagues out of the goodness of the owners' hearts. They had to organise into unions and sometimes take industrial action.

White and the Fertittas are ruthless in deterring any hint that UFC fighters might get organised and collectively demand better terms. Whenever a fighter speaks on this issue he knows White will crack down. The fighters know that to complain is to invite trouble, and most of them are not financially secure enough to risk unemployment. You can't make a living outside the UFC organisation, and you know there are people queuing up to take your place. So you feel you just have to take what you're given.

The only people who could conceivably have the power to challenge the power of White and the Fertittas are the star fighters who drive the PPV sales: people like Ronda Rousey, and now Conor McGregor.

Unfortunately for the Neil Seerys and the whatsisnames, the megastars seem quite contented with the status quo. Rousey recently tweeted a link to a piece from the Las Vegas Review-Journal on the long-running dispute between the Culinary Union and the Fertitta brothers' Station Casinos. It was the sort of anti-union hit-piece you once might have found in the pages of the Völkischer Beobachter.

"Wow. Unbelievable." Rousey commented. The millionaire marshalling her millions of Twitter followers against the kitchen workers who want a better deal from the billionaires who employ her and them.

But Rousey grew up in North Dakota - not a traditional socialist heartland. McGregor is from Crumlin, a constituency that elects Sinn Fein and People before Profit. Remember that first interview with Helwani, and how he wanted to help out his broke-ass Irish brothers? Brash, fearless, supremely self-confident, what better man to lead the fight for a better deal?

So far though, McGregor has cultivated the appearance that he and White are actually friends. There's a video of them roaring down the Strip in White's Ferrari, laughing and shouting into the night. More Molly the mare eating sugar lumps from the hand of Farmer Jones than Big Jim Larkin.

You make your own luck in this game.

McGregor spent the whole week leading up to UFC 189 telling us that the outcome was not in doubt, that he already knew he would win, that he would squash Mendes like a bug, that he would take his little midget head, etc.

I figure a big reason why McGregor says this stuff is to make himself believe it.

He plainly believed he would win, but knowing and believing aren't the same thing. MMA isn't wrestling. It's unpredictable. Shit can and does happen. The Vegas bookies didn't see the result as a foregone conclusion. You could back McGregor at just under evens.

As the lights go down for his ring walk, I still don't even know whether I want him to win. If he loses there'll be a lot of sad Irish people in Las Vegas, but just

imagine getting to hear him justify his defeat.

It seems like three quarters of the Arena is Irish fans and the noise as they await McGregor's arrival is a continuous ear-splitting roar. Hard to believe we're in the middle of the desert 5,000 miles from Dublin. Sinead O'Connor is standing on a pillar belting out *The Foggy Dew*, Celtic mists rising in the Nevada desert, and McGregor's coming in to the Arena. It sounds like the fans know all the words.

Chad Mendes song is *Country Boy*, sung by Aaron Lewis. It's about loving guns and the flag and distrusting big government. He really is a bit of a turkey, is Chad.

Now they're both in the Octagon, McGregor bouncing, Mendes pacing. McGregor is longer and leaner but the stocky Mendes looks more powerful.

McGregor begins the fight by running straight at Mendes and kicking him in the belly. A showy start, but Mendes is watching for the chance to take him to the ground and play to his own grappling strengths.

They're right in front of me when Mendes lifts McGregor off his feet and slams him to the canvas. Now McGregor's on his back and Mendes looks to have him where he wants him. He's working to pin McGregor's body before launching big forearm smashes that come chopping viciously down towards his head. McGregor is cut above the eye and blood is running down the side of his face.

Suddenly McGregor looks pale and skinny and vulnerable. The methodical way Mendes is working reminds me of the dogfight in *White Fang*, when the bulldog locks his jaws on the fur around the wolf's neck and slowly works his grip up the neck, closer and closer to the jugular vein.

It's at this point, identifying him with a favourite fictional character of childhood, that I finally realise I really want McGregor to win. His explanation of how he has inexplicably been defeated will some day be fascinating, but right now I feel I can wait a bit longer to see it.

Later, people who know more about the sport would tell me: Conor was never in trouble. Mendes was never really in that fight. Well, that's not how it looked at the time. The scope MMA offers for tactical and technical talk is one of the reasons for its popularity. But the idea that you can know in advance what is going to happen in a fight, as opposed to making a lucky guess, even the idea that you can know for sure what is happening in a fight while you're actually watching it take place - that is surely a misunderstanding of the nature of fighting. Fighting is chaos. In the end it comes down to intangibles - what's in the fighters, in that moment - things that are impossible to quantify or even to understand.

The second round, Mendes gets McGregor down again, but this time, rather than continue with his methodical elbow assault, he gambles and goes for the submission. Later, he would admit that he was getting tired and felt he needed to finish it before it went to another round.

The gamble is a fatal error. McGregor wriggles free, leaps to his feet, and rains down a series of unanswered blows. With five seconds to go he drives a straight left into the jaw of Mendes. Mendes falls, and the green slopes of the Arena rise to hail the (interim) Champion of the World. Three months later, McGregor made another appearance on

Helwani's show. It turns out that he is agitating with management for a better deal - but only on behalf of himself.

The interview was to celebrate the 300th episode of The MMA Hour. McGregor was returning in his capacity as the show's favourite-ever guest. The tone was a bit different from his previous appearances. In that first interview he was just delighted to be there. Now he adopted the tone of a magnate greeting an esteemed emissary: "Thank you for that great introduction, that is why you are at the top of your game, you can recognise when a man is doing something different and pay him that respect... let's talk."

THE IDEA THAT YOU CAN KNOW FOR SURE WHAT IS HAPPENING IN A FIGHT WHILE YOU'RE ACTUALLY WATCHING IT TAKE PLACE - THAT IS SURELY A MISUNDERSTANDING OF THE NATURE OF FIGHTING.

McGregor's message now is that he is running the game and all the others are fighting over the crumbs that fall from his table. He is a natural in his new role of overdog.

"It's my name that's bringing the numbers, it's my name that's bringing this revenue, so be grateful, recognise it! Recognising somebody that's doing something great, will allow you to do something great. Hating on it, being bitter on it, you're gonna fall!... Don't be bitter, cos you won't get better then! You'll be stuck! You'll be left behind! But... people will be people. They focus on other people instead of focusing on themselves... I can only continue to repeat myself

and try and educate them, but if they don't listen then... FUCK them! I'm still up! I'm still here! I'm still here at the top! I'm still here with the highest paid! Let's compare contracts! Cos now the contract I'm talking Ariel is NINE figures! NINE figures I'm talking! Nobody in the game has talked nine figures! That's one hundred million plus! That's my contract! So that's where I'm at. Learn from it, or don't. That's on you."

It amuses me to imagine how White and the Fertittas might have reacted to these new demands. I get a DM from someone else who's watching this remarkable performance. "Conor might be sleeping with the fishes if he mentions nine figures again."

McGregor and Helwani talked about the UFC fight night scheduled for October 24th in Dublin. McGregor was disappointed that he wouldn't feature on the bill, but nevertheless claimed credit for the fact that it had sold out: "I'll sit and watch the main event that I have built for them."

Economically you could say he's more of a trickle-down guy than a power-to-the-people guy. When one of us goes to war we all go to war - except in negotiations with management.

***

The day after the fight I finished off my work and went for a drink. I had no interest in seeing more of Las Vegas. The city's appeal has a short half-life. Most people are desperate to get out of there after three days and I was on day seven.

CONTINUED OVER >>>

You do a lot of walking around on the Strip. Some of the walks are speeded up by moving walkways which only ever run into the casinos, never out. After walking for a while you begin to notice that there's nowhere to just sit down and chill. If you want to sit, you have to pay - either by feeding money into some gambling console, or ordering something to eat, which in the casinos is always overpriced by a factor of two or three. All of the useless public space has been pared away. Eventually you envy the people on mobility scooters their free seating.

Someone who is just sitting and chilling in the way human beings have done for a million years is wasting Vegas' time, so the Strip is designed to have no resting places. You sit down to have a

beer and you look down to see an electronic blackjack screen built into the bar. It's like the way the lining of the gut is covered in tiny cilia that massively increase the absorptive surface area. That's what the Strip is - a big capitalist intestinal tract that sucks in people, digests them with gambling, strip clubs, booze and drugs, and shits out pauperised human wreckage. It processes and commodifies everything it touches. Conor McGregor is no exception. He's becoming a simulation of himself, with all the cliché big-time accoutrements - shopping and counting, posting videos of his new watch and his trips to Louis Vuitton, driving around in a rented Bentley, making money and spending it on all the things every obnoxiously wealthy young celebrity is supposed to want.

A lot of people have been down that road, and you know who you find at the end of it? Liberace.

The new lifestyle is quite different from the life of relentless work and training that made it possible. There's a saying of Camus' that the struggle itself toward the heights is enough to fill a man's heart. What happens when the struggle is over and you're sitting on the heights with a bunch of designer gear it already bores you to look at?

Is this all there is?

"I love this life, I'm living the dream." He repeats lines like this over and over again.

Maybe he says it to make himself believe it.

terry tries yoga

GOD I'M BORED

go to page 109

PIERCE BROSNAN'S EMIGRANT SHOUT-OUTS
#PBESO

To send us your **#PBESO**,
email editor@secondcaptains.com

ALL NAMES ARE LISTED AT THE BACK OF THE ANNUAL!

SECTION 5

TERRY MONAGHAN HITS ROCK BOTTOM...

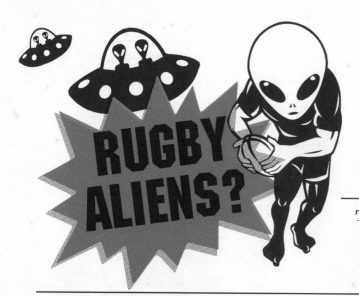

RUGBY ALIENS?

They possess rugby powers from another galaxy, but can you identify the Second Captains RUGBY ALIENS?

Alien 1
Alien Name: Zordan O'Reilly
Position: Second Row

Alien 2
Alien Name: Phantasm
Position: Centre

Alien 3
Alien Name: Mick the Alien
Position: Prop

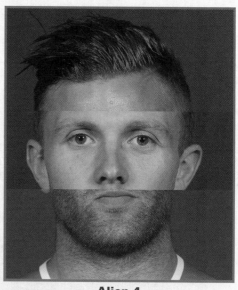

Alien 4
Alien Name: Pretty Boy Zoghorn
Position: Full-back

Hulk Hogan and Andre The Giant - Piper's Pit, 1987: "Take your hands off my shoulders." With those dramatic words, The Eighth Wonder of the World severed his friendship with the Hulkster. Not even Rowdy Roddy Piper's empathetic interviewing skills could save the day as Andre rubbed salt into the wound by literally ripping the shirt from Hogan's back. There was only one place this feud could be settled: WrestleMania III.

The Rockers - The Barber Shop, 1991: Shawn Michaels, how could you?! Sure, the relationship between Michaels and his tag team partner Marty Jannetty had become strained, but we all expected a reconciliation when they appeared together to be interviewed by Brutus The Barber Beefcake. Jannetty offered the olive branch and what did Michaels do? He booted his partner in the head and threw him out through the window of The Barber Shop. The absolute prick.

Hulk Hogan and Macho Man Randy Savage - The Main Event, 1989: The Mega Powers tag team combined Hulkamania with Macho Madness but neither force was strong enough to withstand the green-eyed monster of jealousy. During a match against The Twin Towers, a convoluted series of events led to Macho Man accusing the Hulkster of lusting after his love interest, Miss Elizabeth (The First Lady of Wrestling). During a tense medical room scene, Savage attacked Hogan, creating the animosity that led to an epic bout between the two at WrestleMania V.

The Million Dollar Man Ted DiBiase and Virgil - Royal Rumble, 1991: Calling them men friends might be a stretch, given that Virgil was in fact The Million Dollar Man's much put-upon servant, but they had formed an effective partnership until Virgil decided he could take no more humiliation. As DiBiase stood over him and crowed that "everybody's got a price," Virgil stunned his boss by smashing him over the head with his very own Million Dollar Belt.

Mr. Fuji Betrays Demolition - Survivor Series, 1988: One sneaky flourish of his trademark cane was all it took for this evil genius to eliminate his own team from an incident-packed Survivor Series. Ax and Smash took swift retribution by body-slamming Fuji to the concrete but when The Powers of Pain rushed to his aid in the chaos that followed, it became clear that Demolition had lost their manager to a hated enemy.

SPLIT
HEADS

Examine carefully the split heads and see if you can work out the four GAA players in A, four female Irish athletes in B, and four Irish international footballers in C.

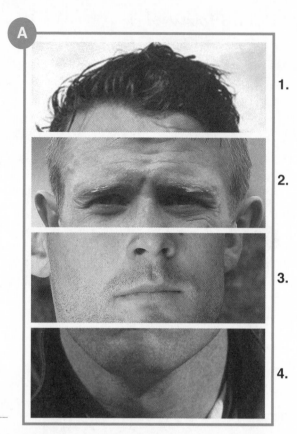

A
1.
2.
3.
4.

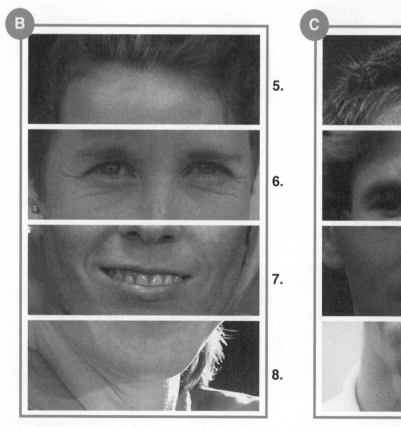

B
5.
6.
7.
8.

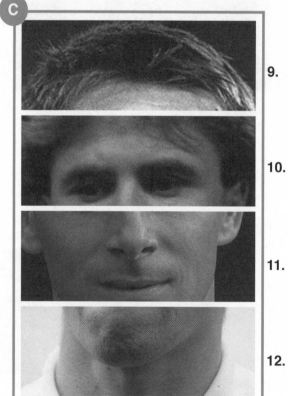

C
9.
10.
11.
12.

```
M  C  L  O  U  G  H  L  I  N
C  G  O  H  A  M  B  O  N  O
G  I  L  E  S  Y  E  D  U  T
R  C  O  Q  A  T  E  A  T  H
A  R  S  E  U  S  F  P  H  G
T  W  A  T  S  I  Y  O  A  U
H  U  G  I  S  M  N  R  I  O
D  A  P  E  Y  T  O  N  R  H
P  A  N  T  S  M  O  I  S  T
G  O  F  U  C  K  M  U  T  S
```

"Can you find the names of 6 former Irish football internationals in our word search? Search for the footballers, stay for the cuss-words!!!"

Scribblebox

TERRY

HAS FALLEN ON HARD TIMES

~RAZZLER'S~

Then

#MADOUTOFIT

GAFFER
THIS IS YOUR LAST chance

GAFFER

This is your last chance

:(I lost my fone gafgwer :(

KEEP SKETCH THERE WILL YOU?

SURE

DO YOU

A DESPITE SOME UPS & DOWNS YOU FIND PERSONAL STRENGTH AND TURN TO GOD 100% JESUS
GO TO PAGE 85

B Continue along this self destructive path?
GO TO PAGE 117

Eoin McDevitt's TOP 5 WWF FINISHING MOVES!

1987-1989

1. 'THE DDT' BY JAKE THE SNAKE ROBERTS

Although technically basic, the slamming of his opponent's head into the canvas was usually sufficient to render Jake The Snake's enemy unconscious. And if that failed, Plan B involved releasing a 15-foot python named Damien into the ring to terrorise his startled foe.

2. 'THE ELBOW DROP OFF THE TOP ROPE' BY MACHO MAN RANDY SAVAGE

As devastating as it was flamboyant, Macho Man's flying elbow brought some of the greatest wrestlers of all time to their knees. His only weakness was Elizabeth, The First Lady of Wrestling, whom he loved perhaps too much.

3.

'THE SHARPSHOOTER' BY BRET THE HITMAN HART

A variation of the legendary figure-four leglock, this submission hold was the most devastating weapon in the armoury of the man they rightly called 'The Excellence of Execution'.

4.

'THE ROCKER-PLEX' BY THE ROCKERS

Forget about their infamous falling out during Brutus The Barber Beefcake's 'Barber Shop' interview, it's best if we all just remember Shawn Michaels and Marty Jannetty for their electrifying aerial ability. Only The Rockers could take a classic individual move like the suplex and transform it into a tag team art form.

5.

'THE SITDOWN SPLASH' BY ANDRE THE GIANT

At a height of 7 foot 4 inches and weighing in at 520 lbs, Andre wisely chose not to overthink things when it came to finishing opponents off. Sitting on them repeatedly would usually get the the job done.

I'm in a bath with Shane Curran… no, actually wait - let's start a little further back.

I'm shooting a promo for the runaway television segment success story of the 2010s, *Challenge Second Captains*, with Shane Curran acting as my (in order of appearance) mafia strongman, gangsta rap chorus member, and, in this particular scene, bath-time companion.

The day had been going swimmingly. Shane Curran may have made his name as a flamboyantly gifted goal-custodian, but he is also a man of boundless patience. He had at various times been wearing a string-vest, a do-rag, and gold chains of dubious quality, and later in the day would spend hours in a French maid's outfit, but nothing seemed to shake the man's innate enthusiasm.

The climax of the *Challenge Second Captains* intro is (obviously) me in a bath, enjoying some me-time when ALL OF A SUDDEN Shane Curran appears from the murky depths at the other end of the bath. The likelihood of him sneaking into said bath without my noticing was non-existent, as it quickly became clear that it had not been built with two burly Connacht gentlemen in mind.

I lit numerous bathside candles, turned down the lights, slid into position and beckoned Shane onto me. He hopped in, a vast displacement covering the bathroom floor in lightly-fragranced bath-water. He could get his backside onto the bath-floor, but there was nowhere for his legs to go. As he playfully booted

BATH
...with Sh

me in the neck and facial area, I suggested he move his right foot over onto the ledge.

A candle had been placed on the ledge, directly underneath an iron hand-rail. Unbeknownst to us, the candle had heated the iron railing to burning point. As Shane manoeuvred into position, he rested his foot on the hand-rail, now a seething cyclindrical instrument of death.

Before the yelp which seemed to come from the depths of hell itself, there was the hiss and sizzle of burnt flesh. Curran thrashed and flailed like the death-throes of the T-1000 in *Terminator 2: Judgement Day*. He f-ed. He blinded. He combined cuss-words in ways I had never heard before. And then – nothing. "Are you… ok?" I asked. "No, I'm fine. I'm fine."

I looked at him. I looked at the crew. They looked at me. They looked at Shane. He wore a face at once pained, and proud. Nothing would bring this man down, not even third-degree burns to his big toe. His exterior seemed to scream – "let's just get this done so I can slip into a pair of black heels, a pencil skirt and a black shirt which accentuates my décolletage, and then we can all go home."

In the autumn and winter of my days, a young cub reporter might have occasion to ask me – "Lord Murphy, what is your definition of professionalism?", and to that fresh-faced young gunner, I will retell the very tale which I have just told you.

TIME

e Curran, by Murph

FIND THE SPORTS STAR!

One of these is a well-known sports PERSONALITY, the other a CELEBRITY. It's almost impossible to identify who's who?

Bernard Brogan Senior OR Artie Ziff

Oisin McConville or T-1000

Denis Hickie or Michael Fassbender

Razor Ramon or Rob Delaney

Richard III or Robbie Robbie Keano

114

1. Who scored Ireland's equaliser against Germany in the 2002 World Cup?

2. Who is Ireland's leading try-scorer of all time?

3. How many European rugby cups have the Irish provinces won, in total, since the start of the competition in 1995-96?

4. How many medals did the Irish boxing team win at the Olympics in 2012?

5. 'Only a Game?' was Eamon Dunphy's memoir of a season with which club?

6. At what Olympics did Sonia O'Sullivan win her silver medal in the 5000m?

7. What county is third in the Gaelic Football All-Ireland senior roll of honour, with nine titles?

8. Who was Ireland captain at the 1999 Rugby World Cup?

9. Name the three Irish starters on the Lions team for the first test against South Africa in 1997?

10. Name the Irish international who appeared in *Escape to Victory*, alongside Sylvester 'Sly' Stallone and Michael 'Michael' Caine?

HOW MANY DID YOU GET RIGHT?

1-3 You have the sporting intelligence of a piece of cabbage

4-6 You are not strictly a disgrace

6-8 You are destined for a life of scholarly isolation

9 You are viewed with suspicion by neighbours for your freakish dedication to #SPORTZ

10 Get back to work Murph, these quizzes are beneath you

GAMEZONE ANSWERS PAGE

#PBESO NAMES FROM PAGES 102-103
1. Cormac O'Connell, Hollywood.
2. Alan, Ayers Rock.
3. Fergus Buckley, India.
4. Neil, Brussels.
5. Barry, Atlanta.
6. Peter, Sinead, Bob, Dearbhla, Boston.
7. Neil, Stephen, Anthony, Alan, Atlanta.
8. Brendan, Oregon.
9. Eoin Corrigan, Ciaran Sherwin, Sydney.
10. Dermot O'Reilly, Cayman Islands.
11. Brian O'Rorke, Fintan Ryan, Tim Mulligan, Shaun Rummy Gavigan, Orla and John, Kuala Lumpur.
12. Neil Fleming, Indiana.
13. Eoghan, Calgary.
14. Shane Horgan, London.
15. Stephen, New York.
16. Conor Long, Melbourne.
17. John Leonard, Peru.
18. Jonathan Dunning, China.
19. Conor Corbett, Patagonia.
20. Cheese Ryan & Derek Jordan, Koh Phangan, Thailand.
21. Niall Mullen, Gateshead.
22. Dr. David Doran, Kilimanjaro.
23. Karl Mannion, Japan.
24. Mary-Claire and Johnny Brennan, Machu Pichu.
25. Garry Doran, Hong Kong.
26. Daryl O'Leary, Myanmar.
27. Warren Maher, South Korea.
28. Sam Hobbs, Lund, Sweden.
29. Redmond Shannon, Madagascar.

To send us your **#PBESO**, email editor@secondcaptains.com.

NSFW IRISH INTERNATIONAL WORD SEARCH ANSWERS:

Internationals: Quinn, McGrath, Houghton, Peyton, McLoughlin, Giles.
Aguable bad-words: Arse, Fucknuts, Twats, Pants, Porno, Ham, Beefy, Pissed, Teat, Nuthairs

SPLIT HEADS ANSWERS:
1- Bernard Brogan, 2- Joe Canning, 3- The Gooch, 4- Eamon McGee, 5- Alan Kernaghan, 6- David Coyne, 7- David Kelly, 8- Chris Morris, 9- Sonia O'Sullivan, 10- Catherina McKiernan, 11- Derval O'Rourke, 12- Fionnuala Britton

RUGBY ALIENS ANSWERS:
Alien 1- Sean Cronin, Peter O'Mahony, Robbie Henshaw.
Alien 2- David Kearney, Simon Zebo, Chris Henry.
Alein 3- Rory Best, Conor Murray, Devin Toner.
Alein 4- Ian Madigan, Keith Earls, Conor Murray.

SECOND CAPTAINS MASTERMIND ANSWERS:
Q1- Robbie Robbie Keano
Q2- Brian O'Driscoll
Q3- 6 (Leinster 3, Munster 2, Ulster 1)
Q4- 4 (Katie Taylor, John Joe Nevin, Paddy Barnes, Michael Conlan)
Q5- Millwall
Q6- Sydney, 2000
Q7- Galway
Q8- Dion O'Cuinneagain
Q9- Keith Wood, Paul Wallace, Jeremy Davidson
Q10- Kevin O'Callaghan

SECOND CAPTAINS YEAR 1 MEMORIES FROM PAGE 101
1. Incredible accurate drawings of Murph by Ken
2. Richie Sadlier WC 2002 callcard
3. Murph at Irish Times photoshoot
4. Collie McKeown presents birthday cake to Mark dressed as gorilla
5. Original garden leave photo
6. Murphpope
7. Shay from Hacienda Bar
8. The local, Fallons
9. #PBESO
10. Frank Sadlier (RIP)
11. Celebrating some good Second Captains news with cans in Trinity
12. Post series in Whelans before Hermitage Green took to the stage
13. @boxgrafik's poster from March 2013
14. Mark Rohan
15. Simon's son Sevvy meets us at our first office
16. Shane Horgan, Andy Lee, Jerry Flannery
17. Our resident goalkeeper Shane Curran
18. Pick of the week in Sunday Times before our first show
19. Brian O'Driscoll poses with the Brian O'Driscoll chair
20. Boom Jayo 95 t-shirt
21. RIP Nelson Mandela
22. An inspirational interview by David Frost with Brian Clough
23. The Clare hero, Shane O'Donnell
24. The arrival of his popeness, Francis
25. Robbie Robbie Keano editing our podcasts
26. Shane and the Gooch in Whelans
27. Donal Og Cusack and Aileen Reid
28. Sonia
29. Bite of Life for sambos
30. Boom Jayo wearing Boom Jayo 95 t-shirt
31. Producer Aideen O'Sullivan pours wine wearing Shane Curran's gloves
32. Post series best looking man competition with Hermitage Green, Jerry Flannery, Andy Lee, Shane Horgan and the self-crowned Murph.
33. Murph as Father Harry Bohan
34. Article from March 2013 predicting our demise!
35. Tetra Delta box
36. Our own Collie McKeown buying the couch we'd eventually use on our set
37. Sensible soccer man (Ray Houghton)
38. The Irish Times retro panini photos of the team
39. Shane and our production manager Karen Reen during intense show de-brief
40. Aideen O'Sullivan in GAA shorts in the office
41. Posing as party Duffer and Keano
42. A loving embrace between Colin Doyle and Ciaran Reay
43. Willie Joe chair
44. Brian O'Driscoll chair
45. David O'Doherty
46. Dog with ball in mouth (no explanation needed)
47. Backstage posing with the greats in RTE
48. Awkward show intro
49. Pat Kenny as a young man (no explanation needed)
50. Pain after New Zealand
51. Our director, the great Maurice Linnane with the Olympic torch
52. Murph as Peter Collins
53. Oisin McConville and Derval O'Rourke
54. Our old rings board from office 1
55. Fergie was still the king
56. Dog with burger in mouth (no explanation needed)
57. ZJD street
58. Rob Delaney backs us
59. Monkeano
60. Jerry Flannery
61. ROG
62. Peter Collins/ Nick Cave
63. Welcome to Jamrock and Damian Marley
64. Nick Cave/ Peter Collins
65. Ken's sick double
66. Liam McHale

SECOND CAPTAINS
WOULD LIKE TO THANK

There are so many people we need to thank for helping us since we started Second Captains in Mark's house in March 2013. Over the past two and a half years, we have met and worked with some truly wonderful and kind people and we're so grateful to everyone who downloads the podcast, and tunes into the TV show.

Thanks a million to Ciaran Walsh and Trevor Finnegan and everyone at Sweatshop and Revert Design for their work on this book and their constant positivity and creativity - you got our nonsense from the start.

To the brilliant Billy Stickland and all at Inpho for their magnificent photography throughout, and to Donal Glackin for his work capturing the last few years in RTE with us.

Thanks to Hugh Ormond, Maurice Linnane, Sorcha Glackin, Elaine McDevitt, Ger Armstrong, David O'Doherty, Conor Purcell, and our pundit regulars and friends Shane Horgan, Oisin McConville, Richie Sadlier, US Murph and Derval O'Rourke.

Everyone in The Irish Times and RTE for their support and faith and to the Second Captains Live backroom crew since series 1.

To all our mates who have helped out behind the bar, or at least stood around drinking at the bar.

A very, very special thank you to our partners in crime, the sober Yin to our raging Yang - the indispensables... Aideen O'Sullivan, Karen Reen, and Collie McKeown. We love you.

To our parents, brothers and sisters - we are thankful for the constructive criticism, and we're sorry for our reflexive defensiveness about every aspect of our business you have decided to ask about since 2013! Thanks for backing us so much since the start.

Lastly - to our partners. Your absentee menfolk are eternally grateful for all your support. xx

Ken, Simon, Mark, Murph and Eoin.

First published in 2015 by Second Captains Limited

secondcaptains.com
editor@secondcaptains.com

ISBN: 978-0-9934291

Produced by: Second Captains and Sweatshop Media
Designed by: Revert Design
Cover Photography: Billy Stickland from inpho.ie
David O'Doherty photography (including pages 28 and 52) by Alex Sheridan
Illustrations by Colm Mac Athlaoich, David Squires
Edited by Mark Horgan
Creative Direction by Ciaran Walsh

Writing from: Ken Early, Simon Hick, Mark Horgan, Eoin McDevitt, Ciaran Murphy,
Brian Murphy and Amy O'Connor.